INTEGRATED ENGLISH

A Course in English Language and Literature

George Wiley
and
Mary Dunk

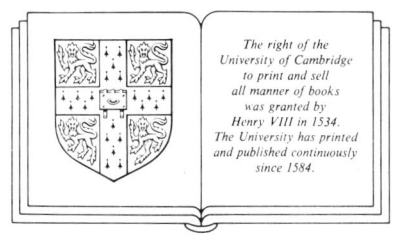

CAMBRIDGE UNIVERSITY PRESS

Cambridge
London   New York   New Rochelle
Melbourne   Sydney

Published by the Press Syndicate of the University of Cambridge
The Pitt Building, Trumpington Street, Cambridge CB2 1RP
32 East 57th Street, New York, NY 10022, USA
10 Stamford Road, Oakleigh, Melbourne 3166, Australia

© Cambridge University Press 1985

First published 1985
Fourth printing 1987

Printed in Great Britain by Scotprint Ltd, Musselburgh, Scotland

ISBN 0 521 27517 2

Acknowledgement
We would like to thank all those teachers and students who offered advice and who helped with the testing of this material. We are particularly grateful to John Carrington of Taunton School, and Jonathan, aged 14 when the work was begun, whose reactions to proposed material and questions were so valuable.

The authors and publishers are grateful to the copyright holders for permission to reproduce the following poetry and prose.

The Hitch-Hiker from *The Wonderful World of Henry Sugar* by Roald Dahl (Cape); extract from *The Roses of Eyam* by Don Taylor (Samual French); Harrison Bergeron from *Welcome to the Monkey House* (Cape); A Science Fiction Story from *Streamline English: Connections* by Bernard Hartley and Peter Viney © Oxford University Press 1979, by permission of Oxford University Press; the estate of Pablo Neruda for Lazybones from *Selected Poems* ed. Nathaniel Tarn, this poem trans. Alastair Reid (Cape); George from *Complete Verse* by Hilaire Belloc (Gerald Duckworth); The Little Girl and the Wolf from *Vintage Thurber* by James Thurber (Hamish Hamilton) © The collection 1963 Hamish Hamilton; Kettlewell is taken from *AA Book of British Villages* copyright © 1980 Drive Publications Ltd, used with permission; the estate of the late Sonia Brownell Orwell and Martin Secker & Warburg Ltd for the extract from *The Road to Wigan Pier* by George Orwell; extract from *Life on Earth* by David Attenborough (William Collins Sons and British Broadcasting Corporation 1979); A Horse and Two Goats from *A Horse and Two Goats* by R.K. Narayan (Bodley Head); Gesture from *Get the Message* by Helen Astley (Cambridge University Press); The Pigeon Cree by Sid Chaplin from *North Country Stories* ed. A.G. Brooks (Faber & Faber); A Black Country Carol by Mary Chitham, *The Black Countryman* 1974, vol 7 no. 1; T' Cure from *Ben Briggs and other Rhymes* by William Beaumont (Advertiser Press); Transglobe by Sir Ranulph Fiennes from *The Observer* 9 August 1982; The Castaway from *Stories and Drawings* by Roland Topor trans. Margaret Crosland and David le Vay (Peter Owen); She lived and 91 others died, Robert Hummerstone/Life © Time Inc. 1972; Soccer Tribe from *The Soccer Tribe* by Desmond Morris (Cape); Shanks for the Golden Memory by Hugh McIlvanney from *The Observer* 4 October 1981; La Divina Pastora by C.L.R. James (*The Saturday Review*); Marriage by Renate Olins from *The Guardian* 12 February 1982; Nicholson Suddenly from *Selected Poems* by Norman Nicholson (Faber & Faber); In Memory of Anyone Unknown to Me from *Relationships* by Elizabeth Jennings (Macmillan); Persons once Loved from *Selected and New Poems 1939–83* by J.C. Hall (Secker & Warburg); extracts from *Living off Nature* by Judy Urquhart (Allen Lane 1980) copyright © Judy Urquhart 1980, reprinted by permission of Penguin Books Ltd; The Holiday and After by permission of the author, Wes Magee; Cathedral Builders from *Requiem and Celebration* by John Ormond (Christopher Davies); Trust by Lynne Reid Banks by permission of Watson, Little Ltd; The Room by permission of the author, Richard Cowen; Colours by Yevgeny Yevtushenko from *Yevtushenko, Selected Poems* trs. Robin Milner-Gulland and Peter Levi (Penguin Modern European Poets 1962) p.77, copyright © Robin Milner-Gulland and Peter Levi 1962, reprinted by permission of Penguin Books Ltd; Learning with Father by Simon Turney from *New Scientist* 30 August 1979; Morning Song from *Ariel* by Sylvia Plath (Faber & Faber 1965) copyright Ted Hughes 1965; People in Prison by Katherine Whitehorn from *The Observer* 6 June 1982; Letter to the British Medical Journal by permission of the writer, Catherine Robinson; Another Day by Hugh Lewin from *Poets to the People* ed. Barry Feinberg (Heinemann Educational Books); extract from *The Green Hills* by Walter Macken by permission of Macmillan, London and Basingstoke; Leeds 2 by James Simmons by permission of Charles Skilton Ltd; An Exaggerated Death by Derek Brown from *The Guardian* 9 October 1982; To the Sea reprinted by permission of Faber & Faber Ltd from *High Windows* by Philip Larkin; The Black Mare from *The Short Stories of Liam O'Flaherty* (Cape); First Blood © Oxford University Press 1963 reprinted from *The Apple Barrel* by Jon Stallworthy (1974) by permission of Oxford University Press; Preludes reprinted by permission of Faber & Faber Ltd from *Collected Poems 1909–1962* by T.S. Eliot.

Photographs are reproduced by permission of the following:
pp 23, 77, 81 Topham; p 50 Barnaby's Picture Library; p 51 Nigel Luckhurst; pp 64, 161 BBC Hulton Picture Library; p 103 courtesy of the Library of Congress; p 145 Kenneth Scowen; p 160 top Sheffield City Libraries; p 160 bottom Sheffield Newspapers.

Designed by Paul Oldman
Illustrations by Annabel Large, Jane Lydbury, Ian Newsham, Paul Oldman and Elivia Savadier
Map by Reg Piggott

CONTENTS

TO THE TEACHER	6

1 ◆ THE SHORT STORY
The Hitch-hiker by Roald Dahl	7

2 ◆ AN ACCOUNT
The Plague at Eyam by George Wiley	20
from *The Roses of Eyam* by Don Taylor	25

3 ◆ MAKING A POINT
Harrison Bergeron by Kurt Vonnegut	27
A Science Fiction Story by	
by Bernard Hartley and Peter Viney	33
Lazybones by Pablo Neruda	34

4 ◆ THE FUNNY STORY
George by Hilaire Belloc	36
The Little Girl and the Wolf by James Thurber	38
The Schartz-Metterklume Method by Saki	39

5 ◆ DESCRIBING A PLACE
Kettlewell from 'The AA Book of English Villages'	46
from *The Road to Wigan Pier* by George Orwell	48
from *Life on Earth* by David Attenborough	49

6 ◆ GETTING THE MESSAGE ACROSS
A Horse and Two Goats by R.K. Narayan	52
Gesture from 'Get the Message!' by Helen Astley	59

7 ◆ WHICH ENGLISH?
The Pigeon Cree by Sid Chaplin	62
A Black Country Carol by Mary Chitham	73
T' Cure by William Beaumont	74

8 ◆ REAL LIFE DRAMAS

Transglobe: three years with fear of failure
from 'The Observer' 76
The Castaway by Rolan Topor 80
She Lived and 91 Others Died from 'Life' Magazine 81

9 ◆ APPROVING AND DISAPPROVING

from The Soccer Tribe by Desmond Morris 84
Shanks for the Golden Memory by Hugh McIlvanney 88

10 ◆ RELATING TO OTHERS

La Divina Pastora by C.L.R. James 92
Marriage from 'The Guardian' 97

11 ◆ LOOKING AT OTHER PEOPLE

Nicholson, Suddenly by Norman Nicholson 99
In Memory of Anyone Unknown to Me
by Elizabeth Jennings 104
Persons Once Loved by J.C. Hall 105

12 ◆ COPING WITH THE WORLD

from Living off Nature by Judy Urquhart 106
The Holiday, and After by Wes Magee 112
Cathedral Builders by John Ormond 114

13 ◆ LOVING ONE ANOTHER

Trust by Lynne Reid Banks 116
The Room by R. Cowen 125
Colours by Y. Yevtushenko 126

14 ◆ THE NEXT GENERATION

Learning with Father by Simon Turney 128
Morning Song by Sylvia Plath 131
Sonnet 19 by William Shakespeare 133

15 ◆ STATING YOUR CASE

People in Prison from 'The Observer'	134
A Letter to the British Medical Journal	138
Another Day by Hugh Lewin	139

16 ◆ SAYING GOODBYE

The Green Hills by Walter Macken	143
As The Team's Head-Brass by Edward Thomas	151
In Memoriam (Easter, 1915) by Edward Thomas	153

17 ◆ A SENSE OF PLACE

Leeds 2 by James Simmons	154
An Exaggerated Death from 'The Guardian'	155
To the Sea by Philip Larkin	161

18 ◆ OVERSTEPPING THE LIMIT

The Black Mare by Liam O'Flaherty	164
First Blood by Jon Stallworthy	171

EPILOGUE

Inversnaid by Gerard Manley Hopkins	174
Preludes by T.S. Eliot	175

◆

To the teacher

This book is intended to help students of a wide range of abilities, aged 14 and above, to read carefully and with understanding; and to use language, written or spoken, with greater awareness of how particular effects can be achieved by a careful selection and structuring of language.

The teaching of English is concerned with enabling students to read with understanding and to write and speak with facility in ways appropriate to a variety of contexts, and this underlying notion is behind the selection of the material included in this book and of the activities which are suggested.

To pursue this objective, the first requirement is that the material itself should be interesting, and we have relied on *complete* short stories and poems. We believe that for the student to deal only with extracts from longer books is dispiriting and if, as we intend, students are to develop their responses to literary texts, there must be opportunity to consider complete works and to think about the ways in which the structure of the whole contributes to the effectiveness of what is written.

There can be no rigid division in teaching English between language and literature, any more than there should be between writing and speaking or between working individually and in a group. Users of this book will find that they are asked to read critically, to analyse what is being said and how it is being said; and to pursue their own creative work, oral or written, in a variety of modes and registers. The book is intended to prepare students for any examination in English Language and Literature, but at no point is any examination objective the explicit purpose of the book.

The material in the book has been widely tested within the age group and everything which did not evoke a positive and favourable response has been excluded. What is included in each unit is feasible and appropriate, though, properly, different groups of students have responded more readily to some kinds of material than to others. Teachers themselves will know when certain of the activities we suggest might be left alone by their particular students or when they should open up areas of enquiry or develop activities based on the material which we have done no more than hint at. Each unit is an entity in itself and although there is a certain amount of cross-referencing, it is unlikely that any teacher will wish to proceed from page 1 to the end.

This is not a class reader, in spite of the considerable amount of 'literature' in the book. The book seeks to stimulate and develop the dialogue between the student and the text, and between students, and to involve the students in their own work. It is certainly not a course book, if that means that it stresses the formal features of writing or speaking which are necessary if one is to measure up to some idea of correctness. Nevertheless, specific direction is given to help students to achieve particular effects of plot, character, description, argument and dialogue in their own work.

We have tried to balance a need for the student to respond on his or her own with a concern for his or her response as a member of a group. In most units there is opportunity for group discussion of issues raised by the material, or for the individual to be involved in some form of group activity. Suggestions are made for other group activities and teachers will doubtless pursue these if and when they are appropriate to their students.

We hope to have produced a book that is stimulating in itself, that is wide in its scope and in which the range of difficulty is far-reaching. The individual teacher will use it as it is appropriate to his or her situation, noting that the suggested activities are such that students will be able to respond at their own level, whether singly, working with a partner, or in a group.

1
THE SHORT STORY

♦

In this story, Roald Dahl, the well-known writer of short stories, tells the tale of the mysterious hitch-hiker who is given a lift by the successful writer. The writer is proud of his success and of his new car. He is very sure of himself and his position, but the hitch-hiker has a few surprises for him.

I had a new car. It was an exciting toy, a big BMW 3.3 Li, which means 3.3 litre, long wheelbase, fuel injection. It had a top speed of 129 m.p.h. and terrific acceleration. The body was pale blue. The seats inside were darker blue and they were made of leather, genuine soft leather of the finest quality. The windows were electrically operated and so was the sun-roof. The radio aerial popped up when I switched on the radio, and disappeared when I switched it off. The powerful engine growled and grunted impatiently at slow speeds, but at sixty miles an hour the growling stopped and the motor began to purr with pleasure.

I was driving up to London by myself. It was a lovely June day. They were haymaking in the fields and there were buttercups along both sides of the road. I was whispering along at seventy miles an hour, leaning back comfortably in my seat, with no more than a couple of fingers resting lightly on the wheel to keep her steady. Ahead of me I saw a man thumbing a lift. I touched the footbrake and brought the car to a stop beside him. I always stopped for hitch-hikers. I knew just how it used to feel to be standing on the side of a country road watching the cars go by. I hated the drivers for pretending they didn't see me, especially the ones in big cars with three empty seats. The large expensive cars seldom stopped. It was always the smaller ones that offered you a lift, or the old rusty ones, or the ones that were already crammed full of children and the driver would say, 'I think we can squeeze in one more.'

The hitch-hiker poked his head through the open window and said, 'Going to London, guv'nor?'

'Yes,' I said, 'Jump in.'

He got in and I drove on.

He was a small ratty-faced man with grey teeth. His eyes were dark and quick and clever, like a rat's eyes, and his ears were slightly pointed at the top. He had a cloth cap on his head and he was wearing a greyish-coloured jacket with enormous pockets. The grey jacket, together with the quick eyes and the pointed ears, made him look more than anything like some sort of a huge human rat.

'What part of London are you headed for?' I asked him.

'I'm goin' right through London and out the other side,' he said. 'I'm goin' to Epsom, for the races. It's Derby Day today.'

'So it is,' I said. 'I wish I were going with you. I love betting on horses.'

'I never bet on horses,' he said. 'I don't even watch 'em run. That's a stupid silly business.'

'Then why do you go?' I asked.

He didn't seem to like that question. His little ratty face went absolutely blank and he sat there staring straight ahead at the road, saying nothing.

'I expect you help to work the betting machines or something like that,' I said.

'That's even sillier,' he answered. 'There's no fun working them lousy machines and selling tickets to mugs. Any fool could do that.'

There was a long silence. I decided not to question him any more. I remembered how irritated I used to get in my hitch-hiking days when drivers kept asking *me* questions. Where are you going? Why are you going there? What's your job? Are you married? Do you have a girl-friend? What's her name? How old are you? And so on and so forth. I used to hate it.

'I'm sorry,' I said. 'It's none of my business what you do. The trouble is, I'm a writer, and most writers are terrible nosey parkers.'

'You write books?' he asked.

'Yes.'

'Writin' books is okay,' he said. 'It's what I call a skilled trade. I'm in a skilled trade too. The folks I despise is them that spend all their lives doin' crummy old routine jobs with no skill in em' at all. You see what I mean?'

'Yes.'

'The secret of life,' he said, 'is to become very very good at somethin' that's very very 'ard to do.'

'Like you,' I said.

'Exactly. You and me both.'

'What makes you think that *I'm* any good at my job?' I asked. 'There's an awful lot of bad writers around.'

'You wouldn't be drivin' about in a car like this if you weren't no good at it,' he answered. 'It must've cost a tidy packet, this little job.'

'It wasn't cheap.'

'What can she do flat out?' he asked.

'One hundred and twenty-nine miles an hour,' I told him.

'I'll bet she won't do it.'

'I'll bet she will.'

'All car makers is liars,' he said. 'You can buy any car you like and it'll never do what the makers say it will in the ads.'

'This one will.'

'Open 'er up then and prove it,' he said. 'Go on, guv'nor, open 'er right up and let's see what she'll do.'

There is a roundabout at Chalfont St Peter and immediately beyond it there's a long straight section of dual carriageway. We came out of the roundabout on to the carriageway and I pressed my foot down on the accelerator. The big car leaped forward as though she'd been stung. In ten seconds or so, we were doing ninety.

'Lovely!' he cried. 'Beautiful! Keep goin'!'

I had the accelerator jammed right down against the floor and I held it there.

'One hundred!' he shouted . . . 'A hundred and five! . . . A hundred and ten! . . . A hundred and fifteen! Go on! Don't slack off!'

I was in the outside lane and we flashed past several cars as though they were standing still – a green Mini, a big cream-coloured Citroën, a white Land-Rover, a huge truck with a container on the back, an orange coloured Volkswagen Minibus . . .

'A hundred and twenty!' my passenger shouted, jumping up and down, 'Go on! Go on! Get 'er up to one-two-nine!'

At that moment, I heard the scream of a police siren. It was so loud it seemed to be right inside the car, and then a policeman on a motor-cycle loomed up alongside us on the inside lane and went past us and raised a hand for us to stop.

'Oh, my sainted aunt!' I said. 'That's torn it!'

The policeman must have been doing about a hundred and thirty when he passed us, and he took plenty of time slowing down. Finally, he pulled into the side of the road and I pulled in behind him. 'I didn't know police motor-cycles could go as fast as that,' I said rather lamely.

'That one can,' my passenger said. 'It's the same make as yours. It's a BMW R90S. Fastest bike on the road. That's what they're usin' nowadays.'

The policeman got off his motor-cycle and leaned the machine sideways on to its prop stand. Then he took off his gloves and placed them carefully on the seat. He was in no hurry now. He had us where he wanted us and he knew it.

'This is real trouble,' I said. 'I don't like it one bit.'

'Don't talk to 'im any more than is necessary, you understand,' my companion said. 'Just sit tight and keep mum.'

Like an executioner approaching his victim, the policeman came strolling slowly towards us. He was a big meaty man with a belly, and his blue breeches were skintight around his enormous thighs. His goggles were pulled up on the helmet, showing a smouldering red face with wide cheeks.

We sat there like guilty schoolboys, waiting for him to arrive.

'Watch out for this man,' my passenger whispered. "Ee looks mean as the devil.'

The policeman came round to my open window and placed one meaty hand on the sill. 'What's the hurry?' he said.

'No hurry, officer,' I answered.

'Perhaps there's a woman in the back having a baby and you're rushing her to hospital? Is that it?'

'No, officer.'

'Or perhaps your house is on fire and you're dashing home to rescue the family from upstairs?' His voice was dangerously soft and mocking.

'My house isn't on fire, officer.'

'In that case,' he said, 'you've got yourself into a nasty mess, haven't you? Do you know what the speed limit is in this country?'

'Seventy,' I said.

'And do you mind telling me exactly what speed you were doing just now?'

I shrugged and didn't say anything.

When he spoke next, he raised his voice so loud that I jumped. '*One hundred and twenty miles per hour!*' he barked. 'That's *fifty* miles an hour over the limit!'

He turned his head and spat out a big gob of spit. It landed on the wing of my car and started sliding down over my beautiful blue paint. Then he turned back again and stared hard at my passenger. 'And who are you?' he asked sharply.

'He's a hitch-hiker,' I said. 'I'm giving him a lift.'

'I didn't ask you,' he said. 'I asked him.'

"'Ave I done somethin' wrong?' my passenger asked. His voice was as soft and oily as haircream.

'That's more than likely,' the policeman answered. 'Anyway, you're a witness. I'll deal with you in a minute. Driving-licence,' he snapped, holding out his hand.

I gave him my driving-licence.

He unbuttoned the left-hand breast-pocket of his tunic and brought out the dreaded books of tickets. Carefully, he copied the name and address from my licence. Then he gave it back to me. He strolled round to the front of the car and read the number from the number-plate and wrote that down as well.

He filled in the date, the time and the details of my offence. Then he tore out the top copy of the ticket. But before handing it to me, he checked that all the information had come through clearly on his own carbon copy. Finally, he replaced the book in his tunic pocket and fastened the button.

'Now you,' he said to my passenger, and he walked around to the other side of the car. From the other breast-pocket he produced a small black notebook. 'Name?' he snapped.

'Michael Fish,' my passenger said.

'Address?'

'Fourteen, Windsor Lane, Luton.'

'Show me something to prove this is your real name and address,' the policeman said.

My passenger fished in his pockets and came out with a driving-licence of his own. The policeman checked the name and address and handed it back to him. 'What's your job?' he asked sharply.

'I'm an 'od carrier.'

'A *what*?'

'An 'od carrier.'

'Spell it.'

'H-O-D C-A-. . .'

'That'll do. And what's a hod carrier, may I ask?'

'An 'od carrier, officer, is a person 'oo carries the cement up the ladder to the bricklayer. And the 'od is what 'ee carries it in. It's got a long 'andle, and on the top you've got two bits of wood set at an angle . . .'

'All right, all right. Who's your employer?'

'Don't 'ave one. I'm unemployed.'

The policeman wrote all this down in the black notebook. Then he returned the book to its pocket and did up the button.

'When I get back to the station I'm going to do a little checking up on you,' he said to my passenger.

'Me? What've I done wrong?' the rat-faced man asked.

'I don't like your face, that's all,' the policeman said. 'And we just might have a picture of it somewhere in our files.' He strolled round the car and returned to my window.

'I suppose you know you're in serious trouble,' he said to me.

'Yes, officer.'

'You won't be driving this fancy car of yours again for a very long time, not after *we've* finished with you. You won't be driving *any* car again come to that for several years. And a good thing too. I hope they lock you up for a spell into the bargain.'

'You mean prison?' I asked, alarmed.

'Absolutely,' he said, smacking his lips. 'In the clink. Behind the bars. Along with the other criminals who break the law. *And* a hefty fine into the bargain. Nobody will be more pleased about that than me. I'll see you in court, both of you. You'll be getting a summons to appear.'

He turned away and walked over to his motor-cycle. He flipped the prop stand back into position with his foot and swung his leg over the saddle. Then he kicked the starter and roared off up the road out of sight.

'Phew!' I gasped. 'That's done it.'

'We was caught,' my passenger said. 'We was caught good and proper.'

'I was caught, you mean.'

'That's right,' he said. 'What you goin' to do now, guv'nor?'

'I'm going straight up to London to talk to my solicitor,' I said. I started the car and drove on.

'You mustn't believe what 'ee said to you about goin' to prison,' my passenger said. 'They don't put nobody in the clink just for speedin'.'

'Are you sure of that?' I asked.

'I'm positive,' he answered. 'They can take your licence away and they can give you a whoppin' big fine, but that'll be the end of it.'

I felt tremendously relieved.

'By the way,' I said, 'why did you lie to him?'

'Who, me?' he said. 'What makes you think I lied?'

'You told him you were an unemployed hod carrier. But you told *me* you were in a highly-skilled trade.'

'So I am,' he said. 'But it don't pay to tell everythin' to a copper.'

'So what *do* you do?' I asked him.

'Ah,' he said slyly. 'That'd be tellin', wouldn't it?'

'Is it something you're ashamed of?'

'Ashamed?' he cried. 'Me, ashamed of my job? I'm about as proud of it as anybody could be in the entire world!'

'Then why won't you tell me?'

'You writers really is nosey parkers, aren't you?' he said. 'And you ain't goin' to be 'appy, I don't think, until you've found out exactly what the answer is?'

'I don't really care one way or the other,' I told him, lying.

He gave me a crafty little ratty look out of the sides of his eyes. 'I think you do care,' he said. 'I can see it in your face that you think I'm in some kind of a very peculiar trade and you're just achin' to know what it is.'

I didn't like the way he read my thoughts. I kept quiet and stared at the road ahead.

'You'd be right, too,' he went on. 'I *am* in a very peculiar trade. I'm in the queerest peculiar trade of 'em all.'

I waited for him to go on.

'That's why I 'as to be extra careful 'oo I'm talkin' to, you see. 'Ow am I to know for instance, you're not another copper in plain clothes?'

'Do I look like a copper?'

THE SHORT STORY

'No,' he said. 'You don't. And you ain't. Any fool could tell that.'

He took from his pocket a tin of tobacco and a packet of cigarette papers and started to roll a cigarette. I was watching him out of the corner of my eye, and the speed with which he performed this rather difficult operation was incredible. The cigarette was rolled and ready in about five seconds. He ran his tongue along the edge of the paper, stuck it down and popped the cigarette between his lips. Then, as if from nowhere, a lighter appeared in his hand. The lighter flamed. The cigarette was lit. The lighter disappeared. It was altogether a remarkable performance.

'I've never seen anyone roll a cigarette as fast as that,' I said.

'Ah,' he said, taking a deep suck of smoke. 'So you noticed.'

'Of course I noticed. It was quite fantastic.'

He sat back and smiled. It pleased him very much that I had noticed how quickly he could roll a cigarette. 'You want to know what makes me able to do it?' he asked.

'Go on then.'

'It's because I've got fantastic fingers. These fingers of mine,' he said, holding up both hands high in front of him, 'are quicker and cleverer than the fingers of the best piano player in the world!'

'Are you a piano player?'

'Don't be daft,' he said. 'Do I look like a piano player?'

I glanced at his fingers. They were so beautifully shaped, so slim and long and elegant, they didn't seem to belong to the rest of him at all. They looked more like the fingers of a brain surgeon or a watchmaker.

'My job,' he went on, 'is a hundred times more difficult than playin' the piano. Any twerp can learn to do that. There's titchy little kids learnin' to play the piano in almost any 'ouse you go into these days. That's right, ain't it?'

'More or less,' I said.

'Of course it's right. But there's not one person in ten million can learn to do what I do. Not one in ten million! 'Ow about that?'

'Amazing,' I said.

'You're darn right it's amazin',' he said.

'I think I know what you do,' I said. 'You do conjuring tricks. You're a conjurer.'

'Me?' he snorted. 'A conjurer? Can you picture me goin' round crummy kids' parties makin' rabbits come out of top 'ats?'

'Then you're a card player. You get people into card games and deal yourself marvellous hands.'

'Me! A rotten card-sharper!' he cried. 'That's a miserable racket if ever there was one.'

'All right. I give up.'

I was taking the car along slowly now, at no more than forty miles an hour, to make quite sure I wasn't stopped again. We had come on to the main London–Oxford road and were running down the hill towards Denham.

Suddenly, my passenger was holding up a black leather belt in his hand. 'Ever seen this before?' he asked. The belt had a brass buckle of unusual design.

'Hey!' I said. 'That's mine, isn't it? It *is* mine! Where did you get it?'

He grinned and waved the belt gently from side to side. 'Where d'you think I got it?' he said. 'Off the top of your trousers, of course.'

I reached down and felt for my belt. It was gone.

'You mean you took it off me while we've been driving along?' I asked, flabbergasted.

He nodded, watching me all the time with those little black ratty eyes.

'That's impossible,' I said. 'You'd have to undo the buckle and slide the whole thing out through the loops all the way round. I'd have seen you doing it. And even if I hadn't seen you, I'd have felt it.'

'Ah, but you didn't, did you?' he said, triumphant. He dropped the belt on his lap, and now all at once there was a brown shoelace dangling from his fingers. 'And what about this, then?' he exclaimed, waving the shoelace.

'What about it?' I said.

'Anyone round 'ere missin' a shoelace?' he asked, grinning.

I glanced down at my shoes. The lace of one of them was missing. 'Good grief!' I said. 'How did you do that? I never saw you bending down.'

'You never saw nothin',' he said proudly. 'You never even saw me move an inch. And you know why?'

'Yes,' I said. 'Because you've got fantastic fingers.'

'Exactly right!' he cried. 'You catch on pretty quick, don't you?' He sat back and sucked away at his home-made cigarette, blowing the smoke out in a thin stream against the windshield. He knew he had impressed me greatly with those tricks, and this made him very happy. 'I don't want to be late,' he said. 'What time is it?'

There's a clock in front of you,' I told him.

'I don't trust car clocks,' he said. 'What does your watch say?'

I hitched up my sleeve to look at the watch on my wrist. It wasn't there. He looked back at me, grinning.

'You've taken that, too,' I said.

He held out his hand and there was my watch lying in his palm. 'Nice bit of stuff, this,' he said. 'Superior quality. Eighteen-carat gold. Easy to flog, too. It's never any trouble gettin' rid of quality goods.'

'I'd like it back, if you don't mind,' I said rather huffily.

He placed the watch carefully on the leather tray in front of him. 'I wouldn't nick anything from you, guv'nor,' he said. 'You're my pal. You're giving me a lift.'

'I'm glad to hear it,' I said.

'All I'm doin' is answerin' your questions,' he went on. 'You asked me what I did for a livin' and I'm showin' you.'

'What else have you got of mine?'

He smiled again, and now he started to take from the pocket of his jacket one thing after another that belonged to me – my driving-licence, a key-ring with four keys on it, some pound notes, a few coins, a letter from my publishers, my diary, a stubby old pencil, a cigarette-lighter, and last of all, a beautiful old sapphire ring with pearls around it belonging to my wife. I was taking the ring up to the jeweller in London because one of the pearls was missing.

'Now *there's* another lovely piece of goods,' he said, turning the ring over in his fingers. 'That's eighteenth century, if I'm not mistaken, from the reign of King George the Third.'

'You're right,' I said, impressed. 'You're absolutely right.'

He put the ring on the leather tray with the other items.

'So you're a pickpocket,' I said.

'I don't like that word,' he answered. 'It's a coarse and vulgar word. Pickpockets is coarse and vulgar people who only do easy little amateur jobs. They lift money from blind old ladies.'

'What do you call yourself, then?'

'Me? I'm a fingersmith. I'm a professional fingersmith.' He spoke the words solemnly and proudly, as though he were telling me he was the President of the Royal College of Surgeons or the Archbishop of Canterbury.

'I've never heard that word before,' I said. 'Did you invent it?'

'Of course I didn't invent it,' he replied. 'It's the name given to them who's risen to the very top of the profession. You've 'eard of a goldsmith and a silversmith, for instance. They're experts with gold and silver. I'm an expert with my fingers, so I'm a fingersmith.'

'It must be an interesting job.'

'It's a marvellous job,' he answered. 'It's lovely.'

'And that's why you go to the races?'

'Race meetings is easy meat,' he said. 'You just stand around after the race, watchin' for the lucky ones to queue up and draw their money. And when you see someone collectin' a big bundle of notes, you simply follows after 'im and 'elps yourself. But don't get me wrong, guv'nor. I never takes nothin' from a loser. Nor from poor people neither. I only go after them as can afford it, the winners and the rich.'

'That's very thoughtful of you,' I said. 'How often do you get caught?'

'Caught?' he cried, disgusted. '*Me* get caught! It's only pickpockets get caught. Fingersmiths never. Listen, I could take the false teeth out of your mouth if I wanted to and you wouldn't even catch me!'

'I don't have false teeth,' I said.

THE SHORT STORY

'I know you don't,' he answered. 'Otherwise I'd 'ave 'ad 'em out long ago!'
I believed him. Those long slim fingers of his seemed able to do anything. We drove on for a while without talking.

'That policeman's going to check up on you pretty thoroughly,' I said. 'Doesn't that worry you a bit?'

'Nobody's checkin' up on me,' he said.

'Of course they are. He's got your name and address written down most carefully in his black book.'

The man gave me another of his sly, ratty little smiles. 'Ah,' he said. 'So 'ee 'as. But I'll bet 'ee ain't got it all written down in 'is memory as well. I've never known a copper yet with a decent memory. Some of 'em can't even remember their own names.'

'What's memory got to do with it?' I asked. 'It's written down in his book, isn't it?'

'Yes, guv'nor, it is. But the trouble is, 'ee's lost the book. 'Ee's lost both books, the one with my name in it *and* the one with yours.'

In the long delicate fingers of his right hand, the man was holding up in triumph the two books he had taken from the policeman's pockets. 'Easiest job I ever done,' he announced proudly.

I nearly swerved the car into a milk-truck, I was so excited.

'That copper's got nothin' on us now,' he said.

'You're a genius!' I cried.

"Ee's got no names, no addresses, no car number, no nothin',' he said.

'You're brilliant!'

'I think you'd better pull in off this main road as soon as possible,' he said. 'Then we'd better build a little bonfire and burn these books.'

'You're a fantastic fellow,' I exclaimed.

'Thank you, guv'nor,' he said. 'It's always nice to be appreciated.'

Roald Dahl

THE SHORT STORY

Suggested activities

1 Working in small groups discuss your reaction to the story and explain why you enjoyed or disliked it. To start with you should consider the following questions.

a Did you like the way the story developed?

b Did you prefer the hitch-hiker or the author, or did your preference change at different points in the story?

c Did you think the hitch-hiker was right to steal the notebooks?

d Did you expect the story to end as it did, or would you have liked it to end differently?

2 It is worth considering the three characters involved in the story. What can you find out about the man who tells the story, the hitch-hiker and the policeman? You may wish to work with a partner. Here are some points which could help you to start your answer.

The narrator Why does he give us all those details about his car? What does that suggest about him? What do we know about his early life? What sort of personality does he seem to have? Does he seem to approve or disapprove of the hitch-hiker?

The hitch-hiker Read lines 23–38 when the man is first introduced and see what is suggested about him. Does his appearance fit in with the impression given of him as the story unfolds?

The policeman He first appears in line 104, and the details given by the author give an impression of the sort of man he is. Which of these details seem important to you, and why?

Discuss your responses to the ideas above, and when you have finished, write one paragraph on each of the characters giving your impression of them.

3 Whilst you were working on question 2, did you notice anything about the way in which the three characters spoke to each other?

a Were there differences in the way each of them spoke?

b Did they alter their style of speech during the story?

For example, the passenger in the author's car became very excited and began to shout when the car was driven fast, but 'his voice was as soft and oily as haircream' (*line 142*) when he answered the policeman. What other examples can you find in the passage of the way in which the characters alter the way they speak?

THE SHORT STORY

4 When you have discussed any points in answer to question 3 make up an imaginary conversation which *might* take place in one of the following situations. Whichever one you choose to write, remember that someone's personality is likely to show through what he or she says. You should try to show how the way they speak changes when the situation changes. If you are not sure how to set out conversation, look at page 44.

a The author meets the hitch-hiker some weeks later in the street. They discuss the incident, but then the author's wife turns up. What is said?

b Two pupils in school are discussing a teacher whom they dislike. That teacher then comes along and interrupts.

c Two truanting pupils are discussing their activities before being seen by the local welfare officer or headteacher. One of these comes along.

d Some shop assistants are overheard by the supervisor who is being criticised by them.

You may think of other situations and other characters, but something should happen which causes them to alter the way they are speaking.

5 The policeman who stopped the speeding driver will have a great deal of explaining to do when he returns to the police-station. His colleagues may not believe that his notebooks really were stolen. Compose the one-page report which he would have to submit to the Superintendent explaining the whole affair. (Think about the sort of language the policeman might use.)

6 Roald Dahl planned this story with considerable care. He 'sets the scene' inside the car, introduces the hitch-hiker of the title and describes the events and conversations which follow. This exercise should help to show how the story is structured.

On a large sheet of paper, draw up two columns, heading one 'Main ideas', and the other, 'Detailed development'. See the table on page 19, opposite. You need not copy down these notes, but, using them as a guide, go through the story and complete both of the columns. Full sentences and detailed comments are unnecessary, but brief notes will show you how the writer

a developed the story,

b leads the reader to the realisation of what the hitch-hiker does,

c finally leads to the climax when the hitch-hiker produces the policeman's notebooks.

THE SHORT STORY

Main ideas	Detailed development
A Introduction	The car. Luxurious interior. Powerful engine. Journey to London.
B The hitch-hiker	Thoughts about his own hitching past. Stopping. First impressions. Huge human rat.
C Conversation	Destination. Character of hitch-hiker emerging. Reluctant to describe his job. Writer admits his profession.
D Speeding	....?

7 Think of a topic which could be developed into a short story using a structure similar to that you have analysed in question 6. Write a brief note about the topic on a piece of paper. (For example, you might write, 'A murder story which involves a skeleton, a map and a safe combination number written on a railway timetable'.) When you have written your brief note about a possible story, fold your piece of paper and put it in a box. Pass the box round the class so that everybody takes somebody else's story topic, then plan an outline based on the suggestion you have picked from the box. List the main events in the order in which they would happen and decide where the climax would occur.

Now write the story.

8 *Further story writing games* If you have enjoyed the activities in question 7, here are some further suggestions.

a Using the topic suggestions from the box, work in groups of four and take turns in writing paragraphs. The first person should write the first paragraph, the second person, the second paragraph, and so on. You will need to be consistent in your use of places and people – if the action suddenly switches from New York to London, for example, there must be some explanation.

When you have all done an agreed number of paragraphs and finished the story, read it aloud to other groups.

b You can play a similar game with titles. The title might be a proverb or saying such as '*A bird in the hand is worth two in the bush*' or '*Look before you leap*'; or you might use newspaper headlines, such as '*Selection Committee blamed for the shambles*', or '*I knew mad axeman*', or '*Granny tells all*'. Make up your own headlines, and then develop the ideas for the story as you did before.

2
AN ACCOUNT

♦

The account which follows tells what happened in 1665 when the inhabitants of the small village of Eyam in Derbyshire fell victims to the dreaded plague. Very many of the villagers died and yet those who remained courageously tried to stop the plague spreading to nearby villages.

The clothes which George Vicars tailored for a living were made to last. He travelled through villages and towns, only stopping long enough in each place for people to be measured, place their orders and have their garments sewn — by hand, of course. He couldn't carry all the fabric and equipment he might need, but he could send to London when he had a large enough order.

He was expecting such a delivery from London in September 1665, while he was still staying in the small Derbyshire village of Eyam. The parcel arrived on September 3rd, addressed to him at the cottage next to the church, where he lodged with a Mrs Cooper.

He unpacked the box and, to his annoyance, found that some of the cloth had got damp on the journey. He hung it round the fire to dry. Within a short while he developed a terrible headache and was violently sick. On the following day he grew delirious and large swellings appeared on his body. On the third day a purple blemish was to be seen on his chest, and he died the next night, September 6th, 1665.

What had caused such a sudden and violent death? Was there some infection within the cloth from London? This proved to be the case. The material had been sent from a city where, only the previous year, thousands of men, women and children had died of bubonic plague. The plague germs were passed on through flea bites, and certainly there had been rat fleas in the folds of the cloth from London which hung round George Vicars' fire. Insanitary living conditions and infestation of rats ensured the spread of the disease.

A bite from an infected flea punctured the skin so that the germs entered the victim's bloodstream, causing swelling to the neck, the groin and the

AN ACCOUNT

armpits. The infection spread within about twelve hours, causing shivering, sickness and headaches. Recovery was possible, but once a purple blemish appeared on the victim's chest, the result of haemorrage, death was unavoidable.

Sometimes the victims imagined there was a sweetness in the air, and excessive coughing and sneezing were common symptoms. The plague was highly contagious, and its progress is recorded in a macabre way in the nursery rhyme:

> Ring a ring of roses
> A pocketful of posies
> A-tishoo, a-tishoo
> We all fall down.

It sounds so innocent, but the 'ring of roses' was the plague spot on the chest, the sign that death was imminent, the 'posies' were the herbs used, somewhat hopefully, as a disinfectant, the sneezing recorded the developing symptoms and the 'we all fall down' acknowledged that death was inevitable.

There had been outbreaks of plague in Derbyshire before, but the plague at Eyam came directly from London where the plague raged in 1664 and 1665 before seemingly being purged by the Great Fire of London. Two facts make the experience of the plague at Eyam extraordinary; one is that out of a population of 350 people, 260 died; the other is the way in which the villagers isolated themselves from all other communities and accepted death rather than risk spreading the disease to others. In London, more people may have died but the community was not destroyed and, terrifying though it certainly was, it was still possible for the majority of Londoners to hope to live and to look on death with some measure of impersonality. In a close community of 350 people, in which everyone would know everyone else, it was surely impossible to watch your relatives and neighbours perish – nearly five sixths of the population died – and to escape personal sorrow or the conviction that your own death was near at hand.

Five months after George Vicars' death, fifty-six people in Eyam had died. Six more died in March, nine in April and six in May. For a brief moment the remaining villagers hoped that the worst was over, but by the middle of the June of that year the plague raged more fiercely still.

The wealthiest of the villagers had already made their escape and a number of children had been got away from the pestilence, but now all who remained were determined to leave Eyam, whatever might become of them. This general resolve to flee by the villagers brought together two unlikely companions, William Mompesson, the young scholarly rector of Eyam, and Thomas Stanley, the former rector who had been replaced in 1660. Stanley had supported Cromwell against the King during the Civil War, as had many

AN ACCOUNT

of the people of Eyam, and he had been replaced as rector when the monarchy was restored in 1660. His continued presence in the village had been an embarrassment to the new rector, William Mompesson, who had come to Eyam in 1664.

The seriousness of the situation brought the two men together, the young scholar who found it difficult to identify with these simple country folk, and the older, more forthright, Stanley. Together, they persuaded the villagers that if they left Eyam now they would spread the disease wherever they went. Perhaps Mompesson and Stanley and Mompesson's wife, Catherine, who refused to leave her husband and the people he served when she might well have done so, are the heroes of this story, but so are all those about whom so little is known, who lived and died at Eyam and who agreed to stay where they were and to endure whatever was to come.

Mompesson wrote to the Earl of Devonshire telling him that the villagers would remain within the confines of the village provided that food and anything else that was needed was provided for them. The Earl agreed to play his part. A circle, roughly marked out by well-known landmarks, was drawn around the village and places on this boundary were determined at which the provisions for the village might be left. One of these places was a well, to the north of Eyam, which is still known as Mompesson's Well. Early in the morning, food was brought from the adjoining villages and left near the well. If any money was involved in the transaction it was placed in the well to clean it. There was no physical contact between those who brought the supplies and those who collected them and took them back to the village.

Mompesson also decided that people should no longer meet in the church, where they could not help but come into close contact with one another. Instead, he held services in the Delph, known as Cucklet Dell, a secluded little spot to the south of the village. But in spite of all the precautions, the plague swept on. Parents watched their children become ill and die one after another. Other children helped bury their parents, until the whole family was swallowed by the pestilence. One poor woman, in a matter of a few days, buried with her own hands her husband and six children. Burial became a perfunctory affair as those still living hastened to get the corpse in the ground before it could spread its contagion.

By the end of August, four fifths of the population had been swept away. Mompesson went from house to house giving comfort as best he could, and with him went his wife Catherine, who had won the hearts of the villagers. Mompesson and his wife were walking in the fields near to the rectory when she is supposed to have exclaimed, 'Oh, the air! how sweet it smells.' Within a few days she was dead.

Another fourteen died in October 1666 . . . and then there were no more deaths. That last remnant, those who had prepared themselves for death, had to adjust to going on living. Thomas Stanley died shortly afterwards.

AN ACCOUNT

William Mompesson moved to Nottinghamshire. Somehow the village revived.

Today you can visit the delightful village and it is difficult to imagine the agony of all those who died three hundred years ago. You can see the cottage to which the parcel of cloth was delivered and where George Vicars died so soon afterwards. Mompesson's Well, Catherine Mompesson's tomb and Cucklet Dell are still there.

Perhaps those who died saved the lives of many others, or perhaps their action was one of foolish self-sacrifice. Yet there was heroism here.

George Wiley

The cottage in Eyam where the plague started.

AN ACCOUNT

Suggested activities

1 Bubonic plague was a catastrophe which could affect any community. You have read what happened at Eyam. First, select the lines from the passage which tell you

   a   what caused the plague to spread,
   b   how the plague came to Eyam,
   c   the symptoms of those who caught the plague.

   Then, using the facts you have identified, write a brief article which could be displayed in a local museum or used in a guide book for visitors to Eyam.

2 William Mompesson remained in Eyam throughout the duration of the plague. Try to put yourself in his position and think carefully how he would have observed the events and what he might have thought. Then write at least three entries in the diary he might have kept. Your entries in the diary could be for three consecutive days or you could select particular times such as

   a   when he first arrived in Eyam – remembering that he was not welcomed by everybody and was himself unhappy at his appointment, or
   b   his reaction to the death of George Vicars, with whom he might have been friendly, or
   c   the time when he realised that it was the plague that was killing the people, or
   d   on the death of his wife, or
   e   when he and Stanley realised that the plague was over.

3 Imagine that you are Thomas Stanley and write a letter to a friend explaining why you joined forces with Mompesson to persuade the villagers to stay. Remember that Mompesson had replaced Stanley as rector of Eyam so that it would not be an easy decision.

4 What do you think the author means by the following?

   a   The plague was highly contagious (*lines 31–2*)
   b   the 'we all fall down' acknowledged that death was inevitable (*lines 41–2*)
   c   the villagers . . . accepted death rather than risk spreading the disease to others (*lines 47–9*)
   d   it was still possible for the majority of Londoners . . . to look on death with some measure of impersonality (*lines 51–2*)
   e   The wealthiest of the villagers had already made their escape (*line 61*)
   f   the young scholar who found it difficult to identify with these simple country folk (*lines 72–4*)
   g   Burial became a perfunctory affair (*line 100*)

AN ACCOUNT

5 The scene which follows is from a play about the plague at Eyam and it presents the moment when the villagers realise that the deaths are being caused by the plague. Read it and, working in small groups, write about another incident in the Eyam story. Write or tape-record your own play. Here are some suggestions, but you may invent your own dramatic moment.

a   The plague is over and the remaining villagers meet.

b   A young man from another village comes looking for his girl-friend, or a young woman comes looking for her boyfriend, after the plague is over.

c   George Vicars receives and unpacks the box of cloth from London.

d   Mompesson and Stanley come together to decide what is to be done when the villagers are determined to abandon Eyam.

EDWARD   Don't go, listen to me!

The crowd ceases its murmur and listens.

Something terrible is happening in our village. One month ago, George Vicars died, with black scabs on his face and chest. Since then ten more people have died in the same way, the last today. Now, are we blind, or children, or what?

WILLIAM   What can we do? People are dying and nobody knows why.

FRANCES   The Rector told Mrs Cooper it's a strange fever from Africa.

EDWARD   You may believe that if you like. But I'll tell you what I think.

HOWE   Listen to the oracle!   10

A burst of laughter from the villagers. Edward Thornley shouts above it.

EDWARD   It's the plague!

The laughter ceases. There is a moment's silence. Then a frightened chatter begins as people start to move off in all directions.

Don't run away like sheep when the dog barks! Listen to me if you want to stay alive!

ELIZABETH   If it's the plague we can't do anything.

MRS HANCOCK   How do you get it?

AN ACCOUNT

JOHN   It's a clammy invisible mist in the air.

GEORGE   You take it in with your breath. You can't do anything about it.

FRANCES   You must carry flowers pinned to your breast. The sweet smell drives it away.

MRS HANCOCK   Is that what they do in London?

JOHN   In London they run away to the country!

EDWARD   If we panic like this we are all dead men.

GEORGE   What can we do?

MRS HANCOCK   We can't do anything, oh God, save us all!

EDWARD   We can act like reasonable Christian men. We can pray to God, and we can take care.

JOHN   What do you mean?

EDWARD   No-one must go near the infected houses, nor touch, nor speak to, nor even look at anyone from them. We must shut ourselves inside with our own families till the danger is over.

Don Taylor

Suggestions for further work

6 It is ten years since the plague ended and you are one of the survivors. Tell the story of what happened to you.

7 You are the first person to enter the village after the end of the plague. Describe what you see and the people you meet.

either

8 Working in groups find out if any disaster ever happened in your own locality and imagine how the people might have reacted. There may, for instance, have been a cholera epidemic, or an area may have been flooded, or there may have been some wartime disaster. Write down the facts of the disaster in historical sequence.

or

The extract from *The Roses of Eyam* suggests something of the fear and confusion which struck the community. Imagine a calamity affecting the town, village or area where you live. If you were isolated with your classmates, for example, how might you respond to tension and danger? Write an account of a fictional disaster which could happen now or in the future, in which *you* are a participant.

9 Explain why you agree or disagree with the conclusion of the account: 'Yet there was heroism here.'

3

MAKING A POINT

♦

Writers often make comments about human behaviour and ideas through their work. Sometimes the comments are obvious; sometimes the point is 'hidden' under the events or characters described. The stories and poems that follow suggest points of view from which to look at human behaviour.

The year was 2081, and everybody was finally equal. They weren't only equal before God and the law. They were equal every which way. Nobody was smarter than anybody else. Nobody was better looking than anybody else. Nobody was stronger or quicker than anybody else. All this equality was due to the 211th, 212th, and 213th Amendments to the Constitution, and the unceasing vigilance of agents of the United States Handicapper General.

Some things about living still weren't quite right, though. April, for instance, still drove people crazy by not being springtime. And it was in that clammy month that the H-G men took George and Hazel Bergeron's fourteen-year-old son, Harrison, away.

It was tragic, all right, but George and Hazel couldn't think about it very hard. Hazel had a perfectly average intelligence, which meant she couldn't think about anything except in short bursts. And George, while his intelligence was way above normal, had a little mental handicap radio in his ear. He was required by law to wear it at all times. It was tuned to a government transmitter. Every twenty seconds or so, the transmitter would send out some sharp noise to keep people like George from taking unfair advantage of their brains.

George and Hazel were watching television. There were tears on Hazel's cheeks, but she'd forgotten for the moment what they were about.

On the television screen were ballerinas.

A buzzer sounded in George's head. His thoughts fled in panic, like bandits from a burglar-alarm.

MAKING A POINT

'That was a real pretty dance, that dance they just did,' said Hazel.

'Huh?' said George.

'That dance — it was nice,' said Hazel.

'Yup,' said George. He tried to think a little about the ballerinas. They weren't really very good — no better than anybody else would have been, anyway. They were burdened with sashweights and bags of birdshot, and their faces were masked, so that no one, seeing a free and graceful gesture or a pretty face, would feel like something the cat dragged in. George was toying with the vague notion that maybe dancers shouldn't be handicapped. But he didn't get very far with it before another noise in his ear radio scattered his thoughts.

George winced. So did two out of the eight ballerinas.

Hazel saw him wince. Having no mental handicap herself, she had to ask George what the latest sound had been.

'Sounded like somebody hitting a milk bottle with a ball peen hammer,' said George.

'I'd think it would be real interesting, hearing all the different sounds,' said Hazel, a little envious. 'All the things they think up.'

'Um,' said George.

'Only, if I was Handicapper General, you know what I would do?' said Hazel. Hazel, as a matter of fact, bore a strong resemblance to the Handicapper General, a woman named Diana Moon Glampers. 'If I was Diana Moon Glampers,' said Hazel, 'I'd have chimes on Sunday — just chimes. Kind of in honor of religion.'

'I could think, if it was just chimes,' said George.

'Well — maybe make 'em real loud,' said Hazel. 'I think I'd make a good Handicapper General.'

'Good as anybody else,' said George.

'Who knows better'n I do what normal is?' said Hazel.

'Right,' said George. He began to think glimmeringly about his abnormal son who was now in jail, about Harrison, but a twenty-one-gun salute in his head stopped that.

'Boy,' said Hazel, 'that was a doozy, wasn't it?'

It was such a doozy that George was white and trembling and tears stood on the rims of his red eyes. Two of the eight ballerinas had collapsed to the studio floor, were holding their temples.

'All of a sudden you look so tired,' said Hazel. 'Why don't you stretch out on the sofa, so's you can rest your handicap bag on the pillows, honeybunch.' She was referring to the forty-seven pounds of birdshot in a canvas bag, which was padlocked around George's neck. 'Go on and rest the bag for a little while,' she said. 'I don't care if you're not equal to me for a while.'

MAKING A POINT

George weighed the bag with his hands. 'I don't mind it,' he said. 'I don't notice it any more. It's just a part of me.'

'You been so tired lately – kind of wore out,' said Hazel. 'If there was just some way we could make a little hole in the bottom of the bag, and just take out a few of them lead balls. Just a few.'

'Two years in prison and two thousand dollars fine for every ball I took out,' said George. 'I don't call that a bargain.'

'If you could just take a few out when you came home from work,' said Hazel. 'I mean – you don't compete with anybody around here. You just set around.'

'If I tried to get away with it,' said George, 'then other people'd get away with it – and pretty soon we'd be right back to the dark ages again, with everybody competing against everybody else. You wouldn't like that, would you?'

'I'd hate it,' said Hazel.

'There you are,' said George. 'The minute people start cheating on laws, what do you think happens to society?'

If Hazel hadn't been able to come up with an answer to this question, George couldn't have supplied one. A siren was going off in his head.

'Reckon it'd fall all apart,' said Hazel.

'What would?' said George blankly.

'Society,' said Hazel uncertainly. 'Wasn't that what you just said?'

'Who knows?' said George.

The television program was suddenly interrupted for a news bulletin. It wasn't clear at first as to what the bulletin was about, since the announcer, like all announcers, had a serious speech impediment. For about half a minute, and in a state of high excitement, the announcer tried to say, 'Ladies and gentlemen—'

He finally gave up, handed the bulletin to a ballerina to read.

'That's all right –' Hazel said of the announcer, 'he tried. That's the big thing. He tried to do the best he could with what God gave him. He should get a nice raise for trying so hard.'

'Ladies and gentlemen—' said the ballerina, reading the bulletin. She must have been extraordinarily beautiful, because the the mask she wore was hideous. And it was easy to see that she was the strongest and most graceful of all the dancers, for her handicap bags were as big as those worn by two-hundred-pound men.

And she had to apologize at once for her voice, which was a very unfair voice for a woman to use. Her voice was a warm, luminous, timeless melody. 'Excuse me—' she said, and she began again, making her voice absolutely uncompetitive.

'Harrison Bergeron, age fourteen,' she said in a grackle squawk, 'has just escaped from jail, where he was held on suspicion of plotting to overthrow

MAKING A POINT

the government. He is a genius and an athlete, is under-handicapped, and should be regarded as extremely dangerous.'

A police photograph of Harrison Bergeron was flashed on the screen – upside down, then sideways, upside down again, then right side up. The picture showed the full length of Harrison against a background calibrated in feet and inches. He was exactly seven feet tall.

The rest of Harrison's appearance was Halloween and hardware. Nobody had ever borne heavier handicaps. He had outgrown hindrances faster than the H-G men could think them up. Instead of a little ear radio for a mental handicap, he wore a tremendous pair of earphones, and spectacles with thick wavy lenses. The spectacles were intended to make him not only half blind, but to give him whanging headaches besides.

Scrap metal was hung all over him. Ordinarily, there was a certain symmetry, a military neatness to the handicaps issued to strong people, but Harrison looked like a walking junkyard. In the race of life, Harrison carried three hundred pounds.

And to offset his good looks, the H-G men required that he wear at all times a red rubber ball for a nose, keep his eyebrows shaved off, and cover his even white teeth with black caps at snaggle-tooth random.

'If you see this boy,' said the ballerina, 'do not – I repeat, do not – try to reason with him.'

There was the shriek of a door being torn from its hinges.

Screams and barking cries of consternation came from the television set. The photograph of Harrison Bergeron on the screen jumped again and again, as though dancing to the tune of an earthquake.

George Bergeron correctly identified the earthquake, and well he might have – for many was the time his own home had danced to the same crashing tune. 'My God –' said George, 'that must be Harrison!'

The realization was blasted from his mind instantly by the sound of an automobile collision in his head.

When George could open his eyes again, the photograph of Harrison was gone. A living, breathing Harrison filled the screen.

Clanking, clownish, and huge, Harrison stood in the center of the studio. The knob of the uprooted studio door was still in his hand. Ballerinas, technicians, musicians, and announcers cowered on their knees before him, expecting to die.

'I am the Emperor!' cried Harrison. 'Do you hear? I am the Emperor! Everybody must do what I say at once!' He stamped his foot and the studio shook.

'Even as I stand here –' he bellowed, 'crippled, hobbled, sickened – I am a greater ruler than any man who ever lived! Now watch me become what I *can* become!'

Harrison tore the straps of his handicap harness like wet tissue paper, tore straps guaranteed to support five thousand pounds.

Harrison's scrap-iron handicaps crashed to the floor.

Harrison thrust his thumbs under the bar of the padlock that secured his head harness. The bar snapped like celery. Harrison smashed his headphones and spectacles against the wall.

He flung away his rubber-ball nose, revealed a man that would have awed Thor, the god of thunder.

'I shall now select my Empress!' he said, looking down on the cowering people. 'Let the first woman who dares rise to her feet claim her mate and her throne!'

A moment passed, and then a ballerina arose, swaying like a willow.

Harrison plucked the mental handicap from her ear, snapped off her physical handicaps with marvellous delicacy. Last of all, he removed her mask.

She was blindingly beautiful.

'Now —'said Harrison, taking her hand, 'shall we show the people the meaning of the word dance? Music!' he commanded.

The musicians scrambled back into their chairs, and Harrison stripped them of their handicaps, too. 'Play your best,' he told them, 'and I'll make you barons and dukes and earls.'

The music began. It was normal at first — cheap, silly, false. But Harrison snatched two musicians from their chairs, waved them like batons as he sang the music as he wanted it played. He slammed them back into their chairs.

The music began again and was much improved.

Harrison and his Empress merely listened to the music for a while — listened gravely, as though synchronizing their heartbeats with it.

They shifted their weights to their toes.

Harrison placed his big hands on the girl's tiny waist, letting her sense the weightlessness that would soon be hers.

And then, in an explosion of joy and grace, into the air they sprang!

Not only were the laws of the land abandoned, but the law of gravity and the laws of motion as well.

They reeled, whirled, swiveled, flounced, capered, gamboled, and spun.

They leaped like deer on the moon.

The studio ceiling was thirty feet high, but each leap brought the dancers nearer to it.

It became their obvious intention to kiss the ceiling.

They kissed it.

And then, neutralizing gravity with love and pure will, they remained suspended in air inches below the ceiling, and they kissed each other for a long, long time.

It was then that Diana Moon Glampers, the Handicapper General, came into the studio with a double-barrelled ten-gauge shotgun. She fired twice,

MAKING A POINT

and the Emperor and the Empress were dead before they hit the floor.

Diana Moon Glampers loaded the gun again. She aimed it at the musicians and told them they had ten seconds to get their handicaps back on.

It was then that the Bergerons' television tube burned out.

Hazel turned to comment about the blackout to George. But George had gone out into the kitchen for a can of beer.

George came back in with the beer, paused while a handicap signal shook him up. And then he sat down again. 'You been crying?' he said to Hazel.

'Yup,' she said.

'What about?' he said.

'I forget,' she said. 'Something real sad on television.'

'What was it?' he said.

'It's all kind of mixed up in my mind,' said Hazel.

'Forget sad things,' said George.

'I always do,' said Hazel.

'That's my girl,' said George. He winced. There was the sound of a rivetting gun in his head.

'Gee – I could tell that one was a doozy,' said Hazel.

'You can say that again,' said George.

'Gee –' said Hazel, 'I could tell that one was a doozy.'

Kurt Vonnegut

Suggested activities

1. When you have read the story discuss with a partner what you liked or disliked about it, giving your reasons for whatever you think.
   Here are some of the things which you might discuss.

   a Did the story seem convincing to you? Did the author make you feel that the events he described could have happened?

   b Do the characters in the story behave like people you know? Even if the characters don't always act like 'real people', does it spoil the story for you?

2. What 'point of view' or comment, do you think that the author of this story is trying to express? Do you agree with it?

3. During the story, the television programme is interrupted for a news bulletin. Make up an imaginary news bulletin to be broadcast later the same day to announce and explain the killing of Harrison and the ballerina.

MAKING A POINT

4 You have been asked to present the story of Harrison Bergeron in comic-strip form. You have been given one page of a comic which will take between 12 and 20 'boxes' or 'pictures'. Working with a partner consider how the story can be shown in these pictures. Sketch out the result and write out any words which will appear with each picture.

5 In the following story the writers recall a very well-known story in order to make a point. Discuss the point you think they are trying to make. Do you think that the writers are successful?

A SCIENCE-FICTION STORY

The spaceship flew around the new planet several times. The planet was blue and green. They couldn't see the surface of the planet because there were too many white clouds. The spaceship descended slowly through the clouds and landed in the middle of a green forest. The two astronauts put on their space suits, opened the door, climbed carefully down the ladder, and stepped onto the planet.

The woman looked at a small control unit on her arm. 'It's all right,' she said to the man. 'We can breathe the air . . . it's a mixture of oxygen and nitrogen.' Both of them took off their helmets and breathed deeply.

They looked at everything carefully. All the plants and animals looked new and strange. They couldn't find any intelligent life.

After several hours, they returned to their spaceship. Everything looked normal. The man switched on the controls, but nothing happened. 'Something's wrong,' he said. 'I don't understand . . . the engines aren't working.' He switched on the computer, but that didn't work either. 'Eve,' he said, 'we're stuck here . . . we can't take off!'

'Don't worry, Adam,' she replied. 'They'll rescue us soon.'

Bernard Hartley and Peter Viney

Further activities

6 When you have thought about this story, try to continue it in your own way, and give your new story a suitable title.

MAKING A POINT

7 'A science fiction story' concerned two people and their spaceship. In the poem that follows, 'Lazybones', the poet has quite a different view of space travel. Read the poem and consider the questions that follow it.

Lazybones

They will continue wandering,
these things of steel among the stars,
and weary men will still go up
to brutalize the placid moon.
There, they will found their pharmacies.   5

In this time of the swollen grape,
the wine begins to come to life
between the sea and the mountain ranges.

In Chile now, cherries are dancing,
the dark mysterious girls are singing,   10
and in guitars, water is shining.

The sun is touching every door
and making wonder of the wheat.

The first wine is pink in colour,
is sweet with the sweetness of a child,   15
the second wine is able-bodied,
strong like the voice of a sailor,
the third wine is a topaz, is
a poppy and a fire in one.

My house has both the sea and the earth,   20
my woman has great eyes
the colour of wild hazelnut,
when night comes down, the sea
puts on a dress of white and green,
and later the moon in the spindrift foam   25
dreams like a sea-green girl.

I have no wish to change my planet.

Pablo Neruda

MAKING A POINT

Further activities

8 Does the poet approve of space exploration?
Look at lines 1–4 of the poem and decide what impression you get of *his* attitude to space travel and exploration.

9 What things in life does the poet seem to value most?

10 Why do you think that the poet says:

I have no wish to change my planet. (*line 27*)?

11 Explain why you agree or disagree with the attitudes of the poet.

12 Write a story in which you visit a planet other than the earth. Think carefully about the comments or point of view you would like to include.

SIMON LANGTON GIRLS SCHOOL
ENGLISH DEPARTMENT

4
THE FUNNY STORY

♦

Funny stories often have a 'moral', that is, they warn us against behaving in a certain way by recounting what happens to people when a particular course of action is followed. The following poem and tale tell us the 'moral' that they each have. In these cases we do not have to work out the warning for ourselves.

You will find both more enjoyable if you read them aloud.

George

Who played with a dangerous toy,
   and suffered a catastrophe of
      considerable dimensions

When George's Grandmamma was told
That George had been as good as Gold,   5
She promised in the Afternoon
To buy him an Immense BALLOON.

And so she did; but when it came,
It got into the candle flame,
And being of a dangerous sort   10
Exploded with a loud report!
The Lights went out! The Windows Broke!
The Room was filled with reeking smoke,
And in the darkness shrieks and yells
Were mingled with Electric Bells,   15
And falling masonry and groans,
And crunching, as of broken bones,
And dreadful shrieks, when, worst of all,
The House itself began to fall!
It tottered, shuddering to and fro,   20
Then crashed into the street below–
Which happened to be Savile Row.

THE FUNNY STORY

When Help arrived, among the Dead
Were Cousin Mary, Little Fred,
The Footmen (both of them), the Groom,   25
The man that cleaned the Billiard-Room,
The Chaplain, and the Still-Room Maid.
And I am dreadfully afraid
That Monsieur Champignon, the Chef,
Will now be permanently deaf –   30
And both his Aides are much the same;
While George, who was in part to blame,
Received, you will regret to hear,
A nasty lump behind the ear.

Moral
The moral is that little Boys
Should not be given dangerous Toys.

Hilaire Belloc

THE FUNNY STORY

THE LITTLE GIRL AND THE WOLF

One afternoon a big wolf waited in a dark forest for a little girl to come along carrying a basket of food to her grandmother. Finally a little girl did come along and she was carrying a basket of food. 'Are you carrying that basket of food to your grandmother?' asked the wolf. The little girl said yes, she was. So the wolf asked the little girl where her grandmother lived. She told him and he disappeared into the wood. When the little girl opened the door of her grandmother's house she saw that there was somebody in bed with a nightcap and nightgown on. She had approached no nearer than twenty five feet from the bed when she saw that it was not her grandmother but the wolf, for even in a nightcap a wolf does not look like your grandmother. So the little girl took an automatic out of her basket and shot the wolf dead.

Moral

It is not so easy to fool little girls nowadays as it used to be.

James Thurber

Suggested activities

1 Both the poem and the tale deal with death. The deaths in the poem are accidental, the killing in the tale is deliberate. Why are they both still funny?

2 Write a story or a poem which has a moral. Make it as amusing as you can.
   Here are some suggestions which may help you:

Someone too young to know any better has a dangerous item. (Rat poison, medical pills which look like sweets, an air gun, a pen-knife with fourteen attachments, and so on.)

or

Something potentially dangerous or awkward happens through carelessness. What are the results? (Uncle Roger, on the top floor of a block of flats, leaves the bath tap running when he goes out, or little Wilfred is left with his deaf Granny and a do-it-yourself chemistry kit.)

or

You could take *a well-known tale and re-tell it in your own way* making it amusing.

If you decide *to write a poem*, you may find it helpful to start with lines which could rhyme easily, for example
   Hannah waved her spanner
   In no uncertain manner . . .

THE FUNNY STORY

The following short story, 'The Schartz-Metterklume Method', has a different kind of humour, which is less obvious because of the style in which it is written and the use of rather long sentences.

Read the story in a small group taking it in turns to read different paragraphs and sections. Discuss any parts or words which you find hard to understand. The main characters are:

Lady Carlotta, Mrs Quabarl, Mr Quabarl, Miss Hope, the children, and the story revolves around a case of mistaken identity.

THE SCHARTZ-METTERKLUME METHOD

Lady Carlotta stepped out on to the platform of the small wayside station and took a turn or two up and down its uninteresting length, to kill time till the train should be pleased to proceed on its way. Then, in the roadway beyond, she saw a horse struggling with a more than ample load, and a carter of the sort that seems to bear a sullen hatred against the animal that helps him to earn a living. Lady Carlotta promptly betook her to the roadway, and put rather a different complexion on the struggle. Certain of her acquaintances were wont to give her plentiful admonition as to the undesirability of interfering on behalf of a distressed animal, such interference being 'none of her business.' Only once had she put the doctrine of non-interference into practice, when one of its most eloquent exponents had been besieged for nearly three hours in a small and extremely uncomfortable may-tree by an angry boar-pig, while Lady Carlotta, on the other side of the fence, and proceeded with the water-colour sketch she was engaged on, and refused to interfere between the boar and his prisoner. It is to be feared that she lost the friendship of the ultimately rescued lady. On this occasion she merely lost the train which gave way to the first sign of impatience it had shown throughout the journey, and steamed off without her. She bore the desertion with philosophical indifference; her friends and relations were thoroughly well used to the fact of her luggage arriving without her. She wired a vague non-committal message to her destination to say that she was coming on 'by another train.' Before she had time to think what her next move might be she was confronted by an imposingly attired lady, who seemed to be taking a prolonged mental inventory of her clothes and looks.

'You must be Miss Hope, the governess I've come to meet,' said the apparition, in a tone that admitted of very little argument.

'Very well, if I must I must,' said Lady Carlotta to herself with dangerous meekness.

'I am Mrs Quabarl,' continued the lady; 'and where, pray, is your luggage?'

'It's gone astray,' said the alleged governess, falling in with the excellent rule of life that the absent are always to blame; the luggage had, in point of fact, behaved with perfect correctitude. 'I've just telegraphed about it,' she added, with a nearer approach to truth.

'How provoking,' said Mrs Quabarl; 'these railway companies are so careless. However, my maid can lend you things for the night,' and she led the way to her car.

During the drive to the Quabarl mansion Lady Carlotta was impressively introduced to the nature of the charge that had been thrust upon her; she learned that Claude and Wilfrid were delicate, sensitive young people, that Irene had the artistic temperament highly developed, and that Viola was something or other else of a mould equally commonplace among children of that class and type in the twentieth century.

'I wish them not only to be *taught*,' said Mrs Quabarl, 'but *interested* in what they learn. In their history lessons, for instance, you must try to make them feel that they are being introduced to the life-stories of men and women who really lived, not merely committing a mass of names and dates to memory. French, of course, I shall expect you to talk at mealtimes several days in the week.'

'I shall talk French four days of the week and Russian in the remaining three.'

'Russian? My dear Miss Hope, no one in the house speaks or understands Russian.'

'That will not embarrass me in the least,' said Lady Carlotta coldly.

Mrs Quabarl, to use a colloquial expression, was knocked off her perch. She was one of those imperfectly self-assured individuals who are magnificent and autocratic as long as they are not seriously opposed. The least show of unexpected resistance goes a long way towards rendering them cowed and apologetic. When the new governess failed to express wondering admiration of the large newly purchased and expensive car, and lightly alluded to the superior advantages of one or two makes which had just been put on the market, the discomfiture of her patroness became almost abject. Her feelings were those which might have animated a general of ancient warfaring days, on beholding his heaviest battle-elephant ignominiously driven off the field by slingers and javelin throwers.

THE FUNNY STORY

At dinner that evening, although reinforced by her husband, who usually duplicated her opinions and lent her moral support generally, Mrs Quabarl regained none of her lost ground. The governess not only helped herself well and truly to wine, but held forth with considerable show of critical knowledge on various vintage matters, concerning which the Quabarls were in no wise able to pose as authorities. Previous governesses had limited their conversation on the wine topic to a respectful and doubtless sincere expression of a preference for water. When this one went as far as to recommend a wine firm in whose hands you could not go very far wrong Mrs Quabarl thought it time to turn the conversation into more usual channels.

'We got very satisfactory references about you from Canon Teep,' she observed; 'a very estimable man, I should think.'

'Drinks like a fish and beats his wife, otherwise a very lovable character,' said the governess imperturbably.

'My *dear* Miss Hope! I trust you are exaggerating,' exclaimed the Quabarls in unison.

'One must in justice admit that there is some provocation,' continued the romancer. 'Mrs Teep is quite the most irritating bridge-player that I have ever sat down with; her leads and declarations would condone a certain amount of brutality in her partner, but to souse her with the contents of the only soda-water syphon in the house on a Sunday afternoon, when one couldn't get another, argues an indifference to the comfort of others which I cannot altogether overlook. You may think me hasty in my judgments, but it was practically on account of the syphon incident that I left.'

'We will talk of this some other time,' said Mrs Quabarl hastily.

'I shall never allude to it again,' said the governess with decision.

Mr Quabarl made a welcome diversion by asking what studies the new instructress proposed to inaugurate on the morrow.

'History to begin with,' she informed him.

'Ah, history,' he observed sagely; 'now in teaching them history you must take care to interest them in what they learn. You must make them feel that they are being introduced to the life-stories of men and women who really lived –'

'I've told her all that,' interposed Mrs Quabarl.

'I teach history on the Schartz-Metterklume method,' said the governess loftily.

'Ah, yes,' said her listeners, thinking it expedient to assume an acquaintance at least with the name.

'What are you children doing out here?' demanded Mrs Quabarl the next morning, on finding Irene sitting rather glumly at the head of the stairs, while her sister was perched in an attitude of depressed discomfort on the window-seat behind her, with a wolf-skin rug almost covering her.

THE FUNNY STORY

'We are having a history lesson,' came the unexpected reply. 'I am supposed to be Rome, and Viola up there is the she-wolf; not a real wolf, but the figure of one that the Romans used to set store by – I forget why. Claude and Wilfrid have gone to fetch the shabby women.'

'The shabby women?'

'Yes, they've got to carry them off. They didn't want to, but Miss Hope got one of father's fives-bats and said she'd give them a number nine spanking if they didn't, so they've gone to do it.'

A loud, angry screaming from the direction of the lawn drew Mrs Quabarl thither in hot haste, fearful lest the threatened castigation might even now be in process of infliction. The outcry, however, came principally from the two small daughters of the lodge-keeper, who were being hauled and pushed towards the house by the panting and dishevelled Claude and Wilfrid, whose task was rendered even more arduous by the incessant, if not very effectual, attacks of the captured maiden's small brother. The governess, fives-bat in hand, sat negligently on the stone balustrade, presiding over the scene with the cold impartiality of a Goddess of Battles. A furious and repeated chorus of 'I'll tell muvver' rose from the lodge children, but the lodge-mother, who was hard of hearing, was for the moment immersed in the preoccupation of her washtub. After an apprehensive glance in the direction of the lodge (the good woman was gifted with the highly militant temper which is sometimes the privilege of deafness) Mrs Quabarl flew indignantly to the rescue of the struggling captives.

'Wilfrid! Claude! Let those children go at once. Miss Hope, what on earth is the meaning of this scene?'

'Early Roman history; the Sabine women, don't you know? It's the Schartz-Metterklume method to make children understand history by acting it themselves; fixes it in their memory, you know. Of course, if, thanks to your interference, your boys go through life thinking that the Sabine women ultimately escaped, I really cannot be held responsible.'

'You may be very clever and modern, Miss Hope,' said Mrs Quabarl firmly, 'but I should like you to leave here by the next train. Your luggage will be sent after you as soon as it arrives.'

'I'm not certain exactly where I shall be for the next few days,' said the dismissed instructress of youth; 'you might keep my luggage till I wire my address. There are only a couple of trunks and some golf-clubs and a leopard cub.'

'A leopard cub!' gasped Mrs Quabarl. Even in her departure this extraordinary person seemed destined to leave a trail of embarrassement behind her.

'Well, it's rather left off being a cub; it's more than half-grown, you know. A fowl every day and a rabbit on Sundays is what it usually gets. Raw beef makes it too excitable. Don't trouble about getting the car for me, I'm rather

THE FUNNY STORY

inclined for a walk.'

And Lady Carlotta strode out of the Quabarl horizon.

The advent of the genuine Miss Hope, who had made a mistake as to the day on which she was due to arrive, caused a turmoil which that good lady was quite unused to inspiring. Obviously the Quabarl family had been woefully befooled, but a certain amount of relief came with the knowledge.

'How tiresome for you, dear Carlotta,' said her hostess, when the overdue guest ultimately arrived; 'how very tiresome losing your train and having to stop overnight in a strange place.'

'Oh, dear, no,' said Lady Carlotta; 'not at all tiresome – for me.'

Saki

160

Further activities

3 When you have read the story a couple of times, work in a group to write a brief paragraph describing what actually happens in the story. Then make a list of the incidents that result from the mistaken identity.

4 When you have read it together, prepare to read the story aloud onto a tape recorder. You will need to choose different speakers to read the words spoken by the characters, and one or two people to read the descriptions in between the conversations. Think carefully about the accents and pronunciation which you will use, and of the ways in which you can bring extra meanings to the story through your voices. When you have decided how you are going to divide and present the reading of the story, record it and play it back to yourselves.

5 Lady Carlotta obviously enjoys shocking the Quabarls. (Which line in the story indicates this?) In your own group think about other things she could have said or done which would have upset her 'employers'. Remember it is important that other suggested outrages should be 'in character' and not too absurd; otherwise they won't seem funny.

6 'The Schartz-Metterklume method' is a name, invented by Lady Carlotta, for a way of teaching history so that children act out history rather than reading about it. Discuss whether or not you like this idea, and then see if you can think of an incident or incidents in history which *could* be taught like this. Plan an imaginary lesson for ten-year-olds on your chosen topic, or write an amusing story in which this method plays an important part. You are the teacher. Look at the notes below on how to set out a conversation in writing.

THE FUNNY STORY

7 Make a list of the various social situations you encounter where a certain kind of behaviour is expected, such as in a railway carriage, in a queue at the post office, at a wedding, at a disco.
   What could you do or say in those situations which would be shocking or embarrassing to the other people there, but which would seem funny to an outsider? Use this idea to write a story describing an example of shocking behaviour from the point of view of an amused observer.

◆

Setting out conversation

When you are including conversation in your writing, it is important to set it out clearly on the page. You can then tell immediately which words are part of a conversation and which belong to the description. Follow these guidelines.

a Use a new line for every speaker, even if he or she only says one or two words.

b Indent that line (do not start the line right up against the margin, but leave a space) so that blocks of speech stand out on the page.

c Start each new speech with a capital letter, and remember to use inverted commas, or quotation marks. These marks show the words actually *spoken* by a person, and they should not include the extra details like 'he said' or 'she answered'.

d Full stops, commas, exclamation marks and question marks all go *inside* the inverted commas, because they tell you more about the actual words spoken. They provide information about the tone in which the words were said.

e If you are still unsure where to use speech marks, read aloud the words you have written. You will soon see which words are part of a conversation between people, and which are extra details. Listen to the conversation in your head if you are shy of reading aloud.

When you are writing out parts for characters in a play, you do not need to observe all of the same rules. It is usual to put the person's name in the margin, to show whose turn it is to speak. You do not need to use speech marks, or inverted commas, but commas, exclamation and question marks will still be necessary. A new line will still be required each time a different character speaks.

THE FUNNY STORY

This conversation, which comes from the book *Catch 22*, has been set out to show you how dialogue can be presented. The left-hand example is written as if in a story; on the right, it has been changed into play-script form.

'From now on,' Major Major said to the middle-aged man who took care of his trailer, 'I don't want you to come here while I'm here to ask me if there's anything you can do for me. Is that clear?'

'Yes sir,' said the orderly. 'When should I come here to find out if there's anything you want me to do for you?'

'When I'm not here.'

'Yes sir. And what should I do?'

'Whatever I tell you to.'

'But you won't be here to tell me. Will you?'

'No.'

'Then what should I do?'

'Whatever has to be done.'

'Yes, sir.'

'That will be all,' said Major Major.

'Yes, sir,' said the orderly. 'Will that be all?'

'No,' said Major Major. 'Don't come in to clean, either. Don't come in for anything unless you're sure I'm not here.'

'Yes, sir. But how can I always be sure?'

'If you're not sure, just assume that I am here and go away until you're sure. Is that clear?'

'Yes, sir.'

MAJOR MAJOR From now on I don't want you to come here while I'm here to ask me if there's anything you can do for me. Is that clear?

ORDERLY Yes sir, when should I come here to find out if there's anything you want me to do for you?

Mjr When I'm not here.

Ord Yes, sir. And what should I do?

Mjr Whatever I tell you to.

Ord But you won't be here to tell me. Will you?

Mjr No.

Ord Then what should I do?

Mjr Whatever has to be done.

Ord Yes, sir.

Mjr That will be all.

Ord Yes, sir. Will that be all?

Mjr No. Don't come in to clean either. Don't come in for anything unless you're sure I'm not here.

Ord Yes, sir. But how can I always be sure?

Mjr If you're not sure, just assume that I am here and go away until you're sure. Is that clear?

Ord Yes, sir.

Make sure you know the difference between the conventions of dialogue by setting out one of the conversation exercises already done in both forms.

5
DESCRIBING A PLACE

The following extracts are all describing various particular scenes. They paint pictures in words. In each case you can summarise the facts, the physical details, very briefly; but, whenever we speak or write, it is usually clear to the listener or the reader what our opinion on the matter is because of the 'positive' or 'negative' words we choose. Each of these authors chooses words carefully and makes us see a particular scene in the way he or she wants us to see it.

Held tightly in the grip of the Pennine crags, Kettlewell is a haven of rest for travellers between Wharfedale and Wensleydale, and for climbers and walkers exploring some of the finest parts of the Yorkshire Dales National Park. But for them, the village might have gone to sleep after its heyday in the seventeenth and nineteenth centuries as a market town and lead-mining centre. Its steep surroundings have prevented any sprawling growth, and its buildings still cluster by Cam Beck, near where it joins the River Wharfe.

At the western end of Kettlewell both the Bluebell Hotel, built in 1680, and the nearby Racehorses Hotel have cobbled forecourts and whitewashed walls, contrasting with the natural stone used elsewhere in the village. Across the beck, near the old stone bridge, stands a shop that used to house the blacksmith's forge and has a top-and-bottom divided door. Upstream a

10

DESCRIBING A PLACE

street leads up to Kettlewell's third inn, the King's Head, and its church, built in 1882–5. A carved font is preserved from the Norman church that was there before.

A charming whitewashed house, dating from 1681, stands beside the narrow 4-in-1 road that zigzags north from Kettlewell and into Coverdale, climbing to more than 1,600 feet before the plunge into Wensleydale. From the village, spectacular mountain scenery greets the eye at every turn. The crags of Knipe Scar dominate the western skyline, Top Mere looms to the north, and the 2,309-foot ridge of Great Whernside soars to the east. Kilnsey Crag, three miles south of Kettlewell beside the road to Skipton or Ilkley, is among the most dramatic rock formations in England.

20

Suggested activities

1 As accurately as you can from the material contained in the passage find out:

 a where Kettlewell is situated;
 b the main occupations for which the village was known when it was at its most prosperous;
 c about the countryside around the village;
 d who are the most frequent visitors to the village;
 e what buildings there are in the village.

2 Pick out six phrases which the writer uses to make the village seem particularly attractive. Explain the effect you think he has achieved in each case and say how successful you think he has been.

3 Why do you think the author tells us the dates when the Bluebell Hotel and the whitewashed house were built? Can you find any other details which emphasise that Kettlewell has been there for a long time?

4 The name of Kettlewell comes from the Old English *cetel-wella*, which means 'stream in the narrow valley' (*wella* = stream, *cetel* = narrow valley).

Choose any five towns, villages or cities, including the one in which you live, and find out the origins of the names.

5 A lot of place-names end in *-ton*, *-ham*, and *-chester*. Find out the origins of these endings. Do you know of any other common endings?

6 Explain what you think the author's intention was in writing this passage about Kettlewell. What do you think is the purpose of the book from which this extract is taken?

DESCRIBING A PLACE

The following extract was first published in 1937. It is based on George Orwell's visit to the area of the Lancashire coalfield during a time of mass unemployment.

from The Road to Wigan Pier

As you walk through the industrial towns you lose yourself in labyrinths of little brick houses blackened by smoke, festering in planless chaos round miry alleys and little cindered yards where there are stinking dustbins and lines of grimy washing and half-ruinous WCs. The interiors of these houses are always very much the same, though the number of rooms varies between two or five. All have an almost exactly similar living-room, ten or fifteen feet square, with an open kitchen range; in the larger ones there is a scullery as well, in the smaller ones the sink and copper are in the living-room. At the back there is the yard, or part of a yard shared by a number of houses, just big enough for the dustbin and the WC. Not a single one has hot water laid on. You might walk, I suppose, through literally hundreds of miles of streets inhabited by miners, every one of whom, when he is in work, gets black from head to foot every day, without ever passing a house in which one could have a bath. It would have been very simple to install a hot-water system working from the kitchen range, but the builder saved perhaps ten pounds on each house by not doing so, and at the time when these houses were built no one imagined that miners wanted baths.

George Orwell

Suggested activities

7 Make a list of the **facts** contained in this paragraph. The phrase *a brick-built building* tells us the fact that there is a building of bricks. In the phrase, *an ugly brick-built building*, the world *ugly* suggests to us what the author feels about the building or what he wants us to feel about it.

8 Pick out six words or groups of words which you think suggest unpleasantness. In each case explain why you think the words have this effect.

9 Using the same facts (your list in answer to question 7) re-write the paragraph so that the scene is made to appear less unattractive.

10 In the last sentence beginning 'it would have been . . .' the author is not describing the scene. What do you think he is trying to do in this sentence?

11 What do you think is the purpose of the book from which the extract is taken?

DESCRIBING A PLACE

from Life on Earth

There are few more barren places on earth than the plains surrounding a volcano in the aftermath of its eruption. Black tides of lava lie spilt over its flanks like slag from a furnace. Their momentum has gone but they still creak and boulders still tumble as the flow settles. Steam hisses between the blocks of lava, caking the mouths of the vents with yellow sulphur. Pools of liquid mud, grey yellow or blue, boiled by the subsiding heat from far below, bubble creamily. Otherwise all is still. No bush grows to give shelter from the scouring wind; no speck of green relieves the black surface of the empty ash plains.

This desolate landscape has been that of much of the earth for the greater part of its history. The first volcanoes to appear on the surface of the cooling planet erupted on a far greater scale than any that we know today, building entire mountain ranges of lava and ash. Over the millennia, the wind and rain destroyed them. Their rocks weathered and turned to clay and mud. Streams transported the debris, particle by particle, and strewed it over the sea floor beyond the margins of the land. As the deposits accumulated, they compacted into shales and sandstone. The continents were not stationary, but drifted slowly over the earth's mantle. When they collided, the sedimentary deposits around them were squeezed and rucked up to form new mountain ranges. As the geological cycles repeated themselves for some three thousand million years, as the volcanoes exploded and spent themselves, life in the sea burgeoned into many forms; but the land still remained barren.

David Attenborough

Suggested activities

12 Referring to the contexts in which you find them, say what you understand by the following groups of words.

- a the plains surrounding a volcano in the aftermath of its eruption (*lines 1–2*);
- b like slag from a furnace (*line 3*);
- c bubble creamily (*line 7*);
- d The continents were not stationary (*line 17*);
- e life in the sea burgeoned into many forms (*line 22*).

13 Numbering the points, 1, 2, 3, etc, list the changes to the earth's surface that the author tells us about.

14 Most of the time this author, David Attenborough, is trying to give us the facts and tell us just what happened. However, he does use a number of words or groups of words which

DESCRIBING A PLACE

suggest that the landscape is uninviting. Pick out six words or groups of words that do this and explain in each case how they achieve this effect.

15 Explain what you think the author's intention was in writing this passage. What do you think is the purpose of the book from which the extract is taken?

General questions

16 The picture below is a photograph of Kettlewell. In the first passage you read a description which made it sound very attractive. Now write your own description of the village from the point of view of someone living there who doesn't like Kettlewell and would like to leave.

DESCRIBING A PLACE

17 This photograph is of the River Thames in London. First make a list of the facts, the details included in the picture, and then write a short essay in which you present these facts

   a from the point of view of the boy in the picture,
   b from the point of view of a tourist who has come to London to see the famous buildings.

18 Discuss in a group the places of interest in your area

   a that you enjoy visiting,
   b that you think a visitor to the district would like to see and learn more about.

   Note down the names of the places in both cases. How different are the two lists?

19 Using the details you have included in your answer to question 18b write a brief article (about the same length as the Kettlewell passage) which would attract visitors to the place where you live. Remember that not only the selection of the details is important, but also the descriptive words you choose in presenting the details.

6
GETTING THE MESSAGE ACROSS

♦

The following story is about an encounter between two men, neither of whom speaks the other's language and who come from very different backgrounds. Neither understands what the other says and they do not appreciate the different importance and value which the statue of the horse has for the other.

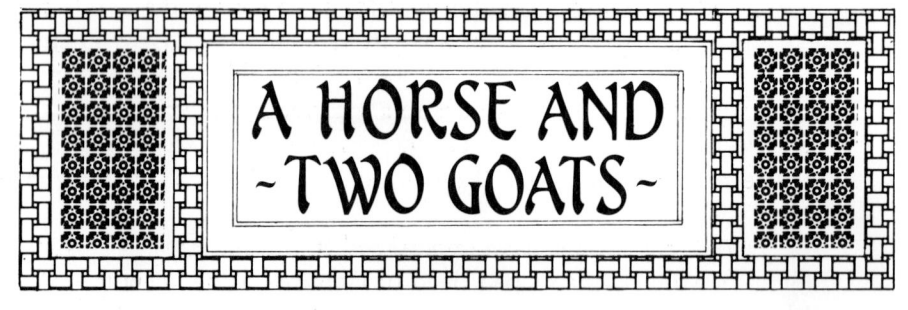

A HORSE AND ~TWO GOATS~

The village was so small that it found no mention in any atlas. On the local survey map it was indicated by a tiny dot. It was called Kiritam, which in the Tamil language means 'crown' (preferably diamond-studded) – a rather gorgeous conception, readily explained by any local enthusiast convinced beyond doubt that this part of India is the apex of the world. In proof thereof, he could, until quite recently, point in the direction of a massive guardian at the portals of the village, in the shape of a horse moulded out of clay, baked, burnt, and brightly coloured. The horse reared his head proudly, prancing, with his forelegs in the air and his tail looped up with a flourish. Beside the horse stood a warrior with scythe-like moustaches, bulging eyes, and an aquiline nose. The image-makers of old had made the eyes bulge out when they wished to indicate a man of strength, just as the beads around the warrior's neck were meant to show his wealth. Blobs of mud now, before the ravages of sun and rain they had the sparkle of emerald, ruby, and diamond. The big horse looked mottled, but at one time it was white as a dhobi-washed sheet, its back enveloped in a checkered brocade of pure red and black. The lance in the grip of the warrior had been covered with bands of gay colour, and the multicoloured sash around his waist contrasted with every other colour in these surroundings. This statue, like scores of similar ones scattered along the countryside, was forgotten and unnoticed, with lantana and cactus growing around it. Even the youthful vandals of the village left the statue alone, hardly aware of its existence. On this particular day, an old man was drowsing in the shade of a nearby cactus and watching a pair of goats graze in this arid soil; he was waiting for the sight of a green bus lumbering down the hill road in the evening, which would be the signal for him to start back home, and he was disturbed by a motorist, who jammed on his brakes at the sight of the statue, and got out of his car, and went up to the mud horse.

'Marvellous!' he cried, pacing slowly around the statue. His face was sunburned and red. He wore a khaki-coloured shirt and shorts. Noticing the old man's presence, he said politely in English, 'How do you do?'

The old man replied in pure Tamil, his only means of communication, 'My name is Muni, and the two goats are mine and mine only; no one can gainsay it, although the village is full of people ready to slander a man.'

The red-faced man rested his eyes for a moment in the direction of the goats and the rocks, took out a cigarette, and asked, 'Do you smoke?'

'I never even heard of it until yesterday,' the old man replied nervously, guessing that he was being questioned about a murder in the neighbourhood by this police officer from the government, as his khaki dress indicated.

The red-faced man said, 'I come from New York. Have you heard of America?'

The old man would have understood the word 'America' (though not 'New York') if the name had been pronounced as he knew it – 'Ah Meh Rikya' – but the red-faced man pronounced it very differently, and the old man did not know what it meant. He said respectfully, 'Bad characters

GETTING THE MESSAGE ACROSS

everywhere these days. The cinema has spoiled the people and taught them how to do evil things. In these days anything may happen.'

'I am sure you must know when this horse was made,' said the red-faced man, and smiled ingratiatingly.

The old man reacted to the relaxed atmosphere by smiling himself, and pleaded, 'Please go away, sir. I know nothing. I promise I will hold him for you if I see any bad character around, but our village has always had a clean record. Must be the other village.'

'Please, please, I will speak slowly. Please try to understand me,' the red-faced man said. 'I arrived three weeks ago and have travelled five thousand miles since, seeing your wonderful country.'

The old man made indistinct sounds in his throat and shook his head. Encouraged by this, the other went on to explain at length, uttering each syllable with care and deliberation, what brought him to this country, how much he liked it, what he did at home, how he had planned for years to visit India, the dream of his life and so forth — every now and then pausing to smile affably. The old man smiled back and said nothing, whereupon the red-faced man finally said, 'How old are you? You have such wonderful teeth. Are they real? What's your secret?'

The old man knitted his brow and said mournfully, 'Sometimes our cattle, too, are lost; but then we go and consult our astrologer. He will go and look at a camphor flame and tell us in which direction to search for the lost animals. . . . I must go home now.' And he turned to go.

The other seized his shoulder and said earnestly, 'Is there no one — absolutely no one — here to translate for me?' He looked up and down the road, which was deserted on this hot afternoon. A sudden gust of wind churned up the dust and the dead leaves on the roadside into a ghostly column and propelled it toward the mountain road. 'Is this statue yours? Will you sell it to me?'

The old man understood that the other was referring to the horse. He thought for a second and said, 'I was an urchin of this height when I heard my grandfather explain this horse and warrior, and my grandfather himself was of this height when he heard his grandfather, whose grandfather . . .' Trying to indicate the antiquity of the statue, he got deeper and deeper into the bog of reminiscence, and then pulled himself out by saying, 'But my grandfather's grandfather's uncle had first-hand knowledge, although I don't remember him.'

'Because I really do want this statue,' the red-faced man said, 'I hope you won't drive a hard bargain.'

'This horse,' the old man continued, 'will appear as the tenth avatar at the end of the Yuga.'

The red-faced man nodded. He was familiar with the word 'avatar'.

'At the end of this Kali Yuga, this world will be destroyed, and all the

GETTING THE MESSAGE ACROSS

worlds will be destroyed, and it is then that the Redeemer will come, in the form of a horse called Kalki, and help the good people, leaving the evil ones to perish in the great deluge. And this horse will come to life then, and that is why this is the most sacred village in the whole world.'

'I am willing to pay any price that is reasonable—'

This statement was cut short by the old man, who was now lost in the visions of various avatars. 'God Vishnu is the highest god, so our pandit at the temple has always told us, and He has come nine times before, whenever evil-minded men troubled this world.'

'But please bear in mind that I am not a millionaire.'

'The first avatar was in the shape of a fish,' the old man said, and explained the story of how Vishnu at first took the form of a little fish, which grew bigger each hour and became gigantic, and supported on its back the holy scriptures, which were about to be lost in the ocean. Having launched on the first avatar, it was inevitable that he should go on with the second one, a tortoise, and the third, a boar on whose tusk the world was lifted up when it had been carried off and hidden at the bottom of the ocean by an extraordinary vicious conqueror of the earth.

'Transportation will be my problem, but I will worry about that later. Tell me, will you accept a hundred rupees for the horse only? Although I am charmed by the moustached soldier, I will have to come next year for him. No space for him now.'

'It is God Vishnu alone who saves mankind each time such a thing has happened. He incarnated himself as Rama, and He alone could destroy Ravana, the demon with ten heads who shook all the worlds. Do you know the story of Ramayana?'

'I have my station wagon, as you see. I can push the seat back and take the horse in. If you'll just lend me a hand with it.'

'Do you know Mahabharata? Krishna was the eighth avatar of Vishnu, incarnated to help the Five Brothers regain their kingdom. When Krishna was a baby, he danced on the thousand-hooded, the giant serpent, and trampled it to death. . . .'

At this stage the mutual mystification was complete. The old man chattered away in a spirit of balancing off the credits and debits of conversational exchanges, and said, in order to be on the credit side, 'Oh, honourable one, I hope God has blessed you with numerous progeny. I say this because you seem to be a good man, willing to stay beside an old man and talk to him, while all day I have none to talk to except when somebody stops to ask for a piece of tobacco . . . How many children have you?.

'Nothing ventured, nothing gained,' the red-faced man said to himself. And then, 'Will you take a hundred rupees for it?' Which encouraged the other to go into details.

'How many of your children are boys and how many girls? Where are they? Is your daughter married? Is it difficult to find a son-in-law in your country also?'

The red-faced man thrust his hand into his pocket and brought forth his wallet, from which he took a hundred rupee currency note.

The old man now realized that some financial element was entering their talk. He peered closely at the currency note, the like of which he had never seen in his life; he knew the five and ten by their colours, although always in other people's hands. His own earning at any time was in coppers and nickels. What was this man flourishing the note for? Perhaps for change. He laughed to himself at the notion of anyone's coming to him to change a thousand- or ten-thousand-rupee note. He said with a grin, 'Ask our village headman, who is also a money-lender; he can change even a lakh of rupees in gold sovereigns if you prefer it that way. He thinks nobody knows, but dig the floor of his *puja* room and your head will reel at the sight of the hoard. The man disguises himself in rags just to mislead the public.'

'If that's not enough, I guess I could go a little higher,' the red-faced man said.

'You'd better talk to him yourself, because he goes mad at the sight of me. Someone took away his pumpkins with the creeper and he thinks it was me and my goats. That's why I never let my goats be seen anywhere near the farms,' the old man said, with his eyes travelling to his goats as they were nosing about, attempting to wrest nutrition out of minute greenery peeping out of rock and dry earth.

The red-faced man followed his look and decided it would be sound policy to show an interest in the old man's pets. He went up to them casually and stroked their backs.

Now the truth dawned on the old man. His dream of a lifetime was about to be realized: the red-faced man was making him an offer for the goats. He had reared them up in the hope of selling them some day and with the capital opening a small shop on this very spot; under a thatched roof he would spread out a gunny sack and display on it fried nuts, coloured sweets, and green coconut for thirsty and hungry wayfarers on the highway. He needed for this project a capital of twenty rupees, and he felt that with some bargaining he could get it now; they were not prize animals worthy of a cattle show, but he had spent his occasional savings to provide them some fancy diet now and then, and they did not look too bad.

Saying, 'It is all for you, or you may share it if you have a partner,' the red-faced man placed on the old man's palm one hundred and twenty rupees in notes.

The old man pointed at the station wagon.

'Yes, of course,' said the other.

The old man said, 'This will be their first ride in a motor car. Carry them off after I get out of sight; otherwise they will never follow you but only me,

GETTING THE MESSAGE ACROSS

even if I am travelling on the path to the Underworld.' He laughed at his own joke, brought his palms together in salute, turned round, and was off and out of sight beyond a clump of bushes.

The red-face man looked at the goats grazing peacefully and then perched himself on the pedestal of the horse, as the westerly sun touched off the ancient faded colours of the statue with a fresh splendour. 'He must have gone to fetch some help,' he remarked, and settled down to wait.

180

R. K. Narayan

Suggested activities

1 Did you enjoy the story? Was it amusing or sad or were you indifferent?

2 Re-reading the story if necessary, notice how it is divided into conversation between the two men, and description about what they are doing and saying. Working with a partner, read out the conversation to each other, taking it in turns to be the Indian or the American. You will have to show by your facial expressions and the movements of your bodies how you are trying to communicate with each other. (For example, the red-faced man is described in line 49 as 'smiling ingratiatingly'. Here they are both trying to show a polite interest in each other without understanding what is going on. There are also other actions mentioned; the American seizes the other's shoulder at one point, and money is later produced.)

3 There are many situations in which people misunderstand each other and their words and actions can be taken to mean something quite different from what they intend. The consequences of such mistakes can be funny, tragic or just unexpected.

Imagine yourself in one of the situations listed below. How would you feel? What might you say? What would you do? What gestures might you make? Would you make friendly signs or look hostile?

a A stranger with a very poor command of English asks for directions by showing a piece of paper with an address. She is in a hurry and behaving oddly.

b You are telling an elderly relative, who is hard of hearing, that you are just going to the post office to get some stamps.

c You are making enquiries about a job over the phone, but the line is bad and neither you nor the employer can make yourself understood.

Work with a partner, and take it in turns to be the people involved in the conversation.

GETTING THE MESSAGE ACROSS

4
a In what ways do you think the statue in the story *used to be* considered important by the villagers?
b What evidence can you find in lines 1–28 which suggests that the statue is no longer considered very important?

5 Explain what you think is meant or suggested by the following:

a The image-makers of old (*line 11*)
b The cinema has spoiled the people (*line 46*)
c uttering each syllable with care and deliberation (*lines 58–9*)
d Trying to indicate the antiquity of the statue (*lines 78–9*)
e he got deeper and deeper into the bog of reminiscence (*lines 79–80*)
f At this stage the mutual mystification was complete (*line 121*)
g The man disguises himself in rags just to mislead the public (*line 146*)
h Attempting to wrest nutrition out of minute greenery (*line 153*)

6 Using a dictionary to help you if necessary explain what is meant by the following words in the context in which they occur.

conception (*line 4*)   astrologer (*line 66*)
enveloped (*line 16*)   deluge (*line 91*)
lumbering (*line 25*)   incarnated (*line 118*)
ingratiatingly (*line 49*)   progeny (*line 124*)
affably (*line 62*)   wayfarers (*line 163*)

7 Remembering the impression you have already formed of 'the red-faced' man, write a letter which he might have sent to his wife telling her how he came to get the statue.

8 The statue has gone. Write or improvise the scene when the old man is questioned about the disappearance by the village headman, who already dislikes him and thinks he stole his pumpkins. (See p.44 for notes on setting out conversation.)

9 In the story 'A Horse and Two Goats' you read about two men who were not able to communicate with each other, not only because they did not speak the same language, but because their backgrounds were very different.
    When we do not speak the same language as another person we rely heavily on gestures to communicate with them. In fact, as the following extract explains, we all use gestures even when we are talking normally, and the meaning of gestures themselves often differs in different countries and different cultures. So even the gestures which the two men might have used could have had different meanings for each of them.

GETTING THE MESSAGE ACROSS

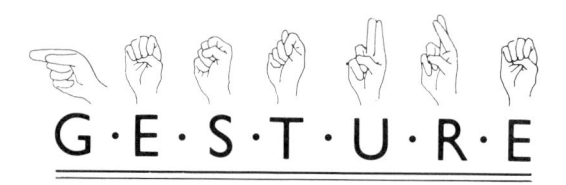

G·E·S·T·U·R·E

Although we are not normally aware of it, most of us use our hands when we are talking. You can see this by turning down the sound on your television set. Notice how much the speakers use their hands as they talk. Our hands can show the shape and size of things (try describing a spiral staircase without using your hands!) and *emphasise* what we are saying. Some gestures, though, have special meanings; what do these people seem to be saying?

These gestures are not made naturally: we have to learn them and they vary from one country to another. For example, how do you call someone to you? In Spain and many other countries you *beckon* someone with your palm *down*, which can look like the English sign for sending someone away. In Italy you wave good-bye with the *back* of your hand which can look like the English sign for beckoning someone!

What do you mean when you nod or shake your head? Nodding seems to be one of the few gestures found in nearly every country; it seems to mean 'yes' almost everywhere but in some parts of India, for example, *shaking* the head *also* means 'yes'. In Greece and Southern Italy and many other parts of the world, throwing the head back, which can look like a nod, means 'no'.

When you see your friends, how do you greet them? People in many countries find the English cold and unfriendly because they often do no more than say 'hello'. Even adults shake hands usually only the first time they meet. French people, including schoolchildren, shake hands with their friends, or kiss them on both cheeks if they are close friends, each time they meet and when they leave one another. At home they do not go to bed without kissing everyone in the family good night, on both cheeks, and shaking hands with any visitors. The same thing happens in the morning.

GETTING THE MESSAGE ACROSS

How do you think a French child might feel staying in your family?

Other countries have different ways of greeting. The Eskimos rub noses. In Samoa people sniff one another and in Polynesia you take hold of your friend's hands and use them to stroke your face. In Tibet it is very polite to stick your tongue out at someone; you are saying 'there is no evil thought in my tongue'!

In some parts of East Africa it is considered very unlucky to point with your fingers and so people turn their heads and pout their lips in the direction they mean. In Britain some people 'cross their fingers' for good luck but in Austria and Germany they hold their thumbs. In Britain, if the people in an audience do not like a performer and if they are not very polite they may clap their hands slowly to mean 'go away!'. In other parts of Europe the slow hand clap is a great compliment! In Britain people may stand up as a sign of respect. In some other countries they sit down to show that they look *up* to the person.

There are many other signs used in different countries, and what is an insult in one country may not be understood or may have quite a different meaning in another. The English do not use gesture as much as many other people and it is very easy for misunderstandings to arise.

Helen Astley

Further activities

10 Working with a partner, plan and act a series of *mimes* showing how people express the primary emotions. These are:

happiness, anger, surprise, fear, disgust, sadness and interest.

You do not need to choose more than three of these emotions, but you should try to do two mimes for each emotion. One mime should be of people in countries where bodily contact is common, and the other of people who do not show feelings through contact. (An example of this might be happiness at seeing a friend after a long absence. 'Body contact' cultures might go in for a lot of hugging and kissing and arm waving, whereas others might just shake hands with a happy smile on their faces.)

11 Make a collection of pictures cut from newspapers and magazines (or which you have taken yourself) that show people communicating emotions through facial expressions and the way in which they move.

Choose one or two of the pictures and use them as the basis for a story or some descriptive writing. (If you have studied Unit 11 in this book, you may have already made such a collection of photographs; you may use this if you wish.)

GETTING THE MESSAGE ACROSS

12 **Charades** is a party game where one person or a small group of people mime something and the others guess the word or group of words. The simplest game gets someone to mime the title of a book, play or film (such as *A Tale of Two Cities* or *Tinker, Tailor, Soldier, Spy*) and the others have to guess what it is.

Divide into groups and play charades. If possible, involve all the group in the mime.

13 You have studied the ways in which people communicate with each other with and without words. It is possible to communicate information without speaking *and* without being seen by the other person or people.

a Working in your groups, each person should draw as many of the Highway Code signs as he or she knows. After a set time, show your sketches to the others and say what is being communicated through the signs.

b You have been asked to design a new crest or badge for your school or the area in which you live. It should not have any words, but should show the main features or activities for which the place is famous.

What would you put on the badge, and why?

14 A down-to-earth problem of communication arises when people from different cultures meet together at something like an international airport. How do you let people know where everything is?

Imagine that the planners for a new airport or railway station have asked you to design signs to represent the various facilities. Most passengers will be unable to read English and they will come from a wide range of cultures and races.

Make a sketch of the signs to represent the following facilities. Explain briefly any special difficulty you have in choosing any of the signs.

- a The car park
- b The enquiries office
- c The bus stop to the local town
- d The post office
- e Bookshops
- f The dining room
- g The bar
- h The toilets
- i The departure gates
- j The taxi-rank
- k The hairdresser
- l The airline offices
- m Meeting points
- n Duty-free shops
- o The left-luggage room
- p Customs
- q Passport Check
- r First Aid

7
WHICH ENGLISH?

The following story, which is set in the north-east of England, is about a man whose hobby is keeping pigeons. This hobby brings him into conflict with his wife and his local council.

THE PIGEON CREE

Upon a green hill in the pit valley there stands this leaning contraption which they call a pigeon cree. It is made up of odd pieces of wood and canvas, and painted all kinds of fancy colours round the sides, the roof being just a plain whitewash to show the birds that this is home. There is a big window running all along one side, and above this window there is a little platform upon which the birds alight before going inside through the tiny trapdoors which Geordie has so kindly provided for them.

Who is this Geordie? Well, he is an old miner nearing the end of his time, not far off pension age, and not caring how soon it's here either. This Geordie works every night, two hundred fathoms down, and doesn't like it. He never did like it. Hated it from the first day he dropped into the blackness. He doesn't like the heat, the dust, the dark or the work itself; he likes only the weekly paynote, and the wife gets most of that — she takes good care she does.

His only compensation is this cree (which is our word for shed) and these birds, his pigeons, some being tumblers, stragglers, tame 'uns from the woods and straight racing birds which have won him many prizes and not a few bets. He loves all his birds alike, no favourites, and they in turn respect this small bandy-legged bloke that sets them a-flying, feeds them corn and whistles them in before nightfall.

Now it chances one morning upon this green hill, while Geordie is watching his birds tumble and swoop in the blue, that a feller from the local council offices puffs his way up to the cree. This feller is named John William

WHICH ENGLISH?

Thwaites, and he's clerk to the council, which is a pretty important job in his estimation. Now old Geordie doesn't observe this feller till he's almost up, which is a pity, for he guesses what he's coming about. But just to annoy John Willy he pretends to be more interested in the antics of his birds than the puffings an' blowings of a sourpuss of a council clerk.

"Hey," sez John Willy in a local-authority tone of voice.

"Morning, John Willy me lad," sez Geordie, and spits, just missing John Willy's cherried shoes, now up to the tops in muck.

"I've come about this shed of yours. The council passed a minute last night prohibiting such things in council-owned allotments."

"Shed?" sez Geordie. "If Ah remember reet ye used ter call them crees, same as me, when yer — when ye was a lad. And as fer prohibition, it didn't work in Yankeeland, an' it won't work here either."

"What the council passes is law," answered John Willy.

"When Parlyment passes that Geordie Howell can't keep pigeons in his own cree, then Ah'll sit up and take notice," sez Geordie, and starts knocking the dottle out of his old pipe, which shows he's getting all het-up and a bad time coming for John William Thwaites.

"Now, my good man, look here . . ."

"Dinna tha 'good man' me," shouts Geordie, "or Ah'll spank thee arse, an' hard at that!"

John Willy goes all white and shaky, then red as a turkey as he sez: "I'll bring the police to you, and then we'll see what you have to say."

"Tha'll bring the whole force if tha likes, but here Ah am, and here Ah intend ter stay. And tha can tell the council that. Aye, an' the slops if tha wants."

"That's the height of impudence," sez the clerk. "I can't take a message like that back to the councillors."

"It might waken them up a bit," sez Geordie. And he starts whistling his birds in for lunch, signifying by this that the interview is at an end. John Willy sees that it's a hopeless job he's got, so he snorts, pulls down his trilby, and scrams with all the dignity he can muster. And the old man starts scattering corn for the birds, laughing as he sees them peeking away like pneumatic picks with a few feathers stuck on, if you see what I mean. For Geordie loves his birds. He doesn't really keep them for racing and winning prizes. This flying is still a miracle to him. When he was a kid he gazed at birds in the air with a kind of amazement. He wanted to join the big white gulls flying after the ploughs, the crested peewits, the blue pigeons. He works two hundred fathoms down, but his mind is always with the winds and the wide-winged birds. He's a shifter and goes down the mine every day at five, but before the steel cage drops like a torpedo into darkness his eyes turn to the sky in the hope that a bird might swim into view.

Now this is one of the mornings when coincidences happen by the hour

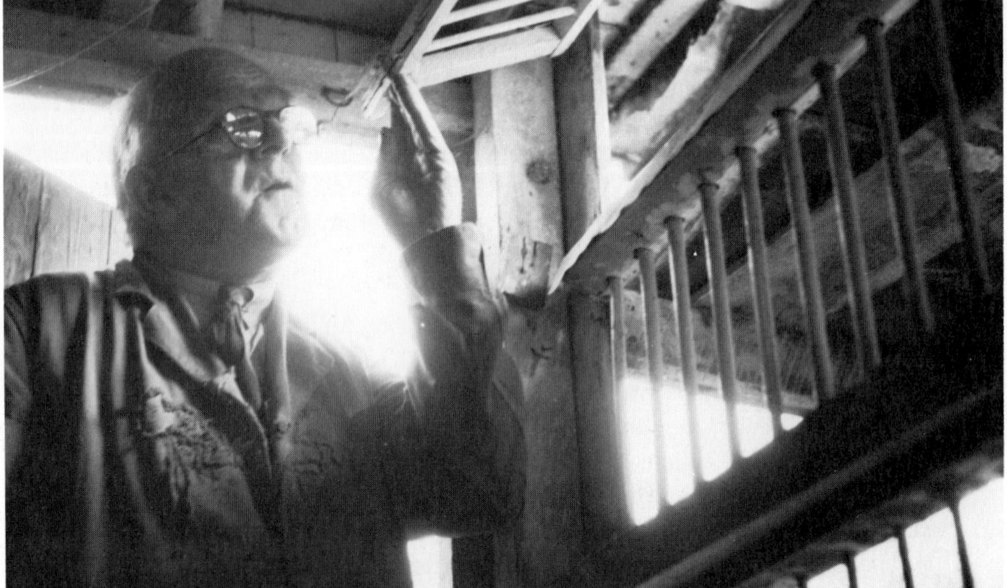

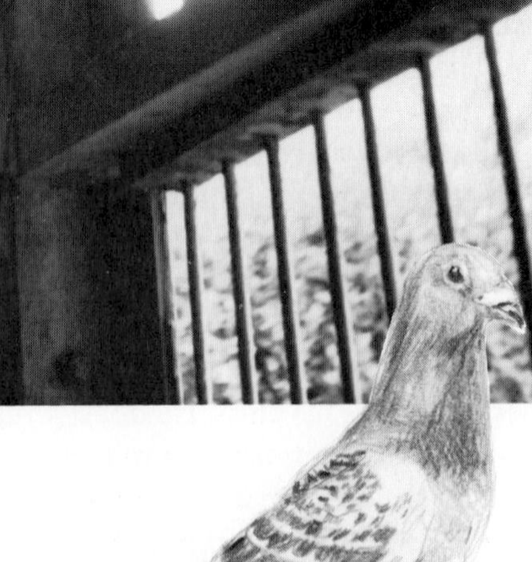

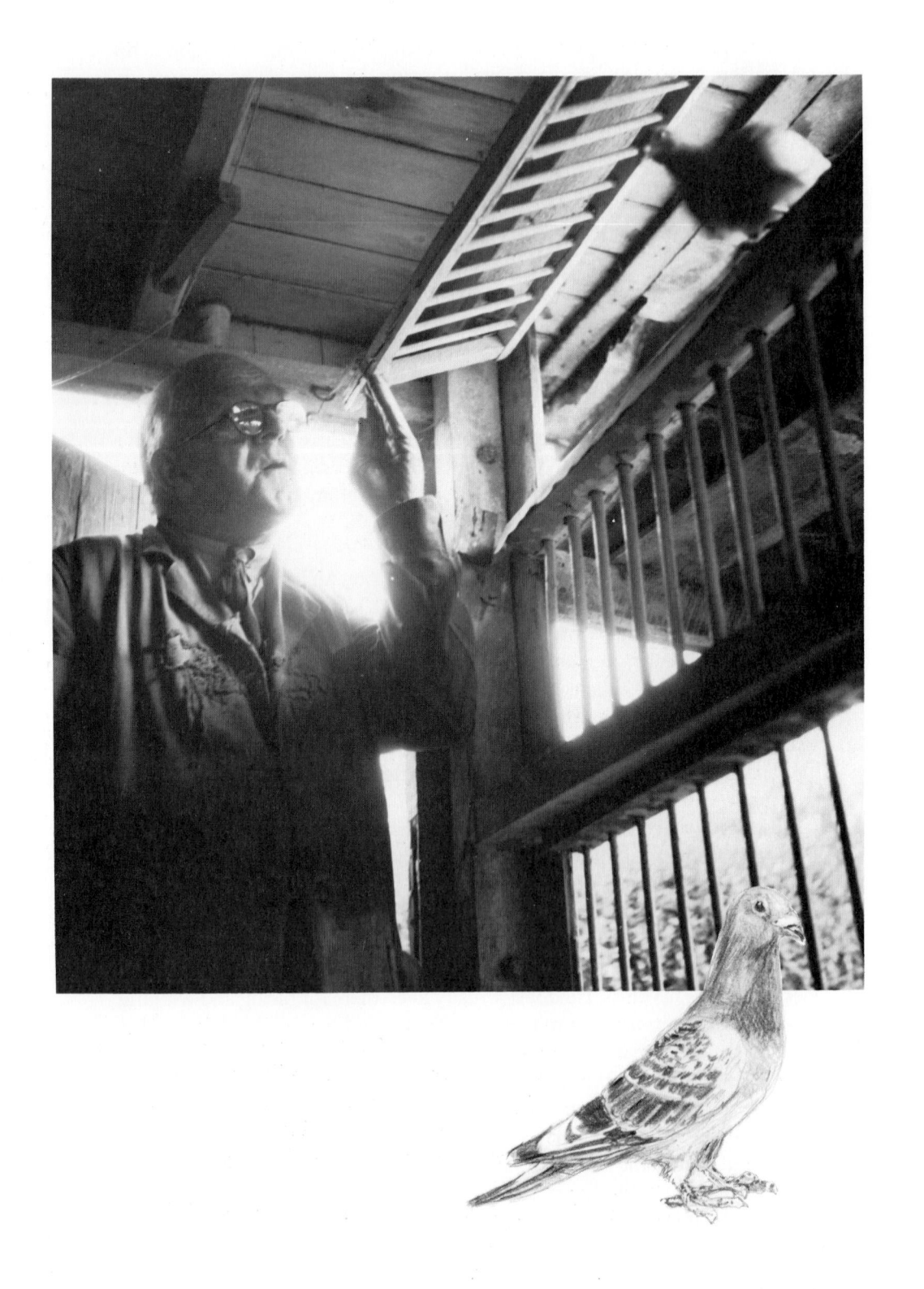

WHICH ENGLISH?

and the score. Men, like creeping things and dumb beasts, are drawn outside by the sun. And this morning the sun shines direct upon the glass window of the pigeon cree and is reflected, like the flash of a sword, into the determined eyes of the Reverend James Aloysis Jefferies, who is the local puritan, and no mistake about that. Now, Geordie's missis paid a visit to same last week and told him how she detests this ancient crazy shed which leads her husband into the paths of sin and the way of the devil, seeing that he keeps therein certain birds which fly races for sums of money; it was a sin, and she a respectable woman who has been trying to save her husband many years, but he's a hardened case and the devil's got his talons deep.

Now this flash in the eye reminds the Reverend that he has a task to accomplish, for he promised Geordie's wife that, with the help of the Lord, the sinner would be led like a shorn lamb into the congregation of the saints and the paths of righteousness. Amen. So he rises from his comfortable seat, carefully places a chewed match as bookmark into the yellowback he has been reading, and makes for the hill.

Now, he comes upon Geordie unawares. The bandy-legged old man is silent upon his prayers. He is leaning against the front of the cree, gazing into the sky. The object of his devotion is a young bird, free for the first time. Drunk with warmth of the sun, the power surging in his young wings, and the discovery of a thousand invisible currents and eddies, he is whirling and sweeping and hovering in the free air, uttering half-inarticulate cries of joy.

"Good morning, Mister Howell," he sez, kind of snappy.

Geordie looks at him, a bit dazed and surprised. The young bird sweeps down, uttering exultant cries, and Geordie's eyes have to follow. Somehow the Reverend is caught by that look. He weakens, then remembers that business is business.

"It's a long time since I last saw you," he sez firmly. "I thought I would take advantage of this sunshine – God's sunshine – and make this long-deferred visit."

"Kind of you," sez Geordie. "Grand day, isn't it? Makes you feel glad to be alive – like yon young bird there. He's a bit drunk wi'it, though."

"Oh, the pigeon . . ." sez the Reverend contemptuously.

"My philosophy is that the sun shines fer birds as well as men," sez the old man.

"Now, Mister Howell, you can't compare a mere bird with man! You'll be telling me next they have a part in God's plan of salvation. Granted they have a part in the creation, but not as racing birds. When the good Lord created pigeons he meant them for anything but racing."

"When God created horses He meant them fer anything but huntin', but that didn't stop John Wesley frae riding one," sez Geordie.

"That's different," sez the Rev.

"Fer your agyment," sez Geordie. "But it's true, arl the same."

WHICH ENGLISH?

"I'll come to the point," sez the parson.

"Yer needn't bother," sez Geordie. "Ah'm not as green as Ah'm cabbage-looking. Yer want ter stop me keeping pigeons, just the same as yer want ter stop others frae ganning ter the pictures or drinkin' beer. You want iverbody ter be the same as you, which, beggin' yer pardon, would be a big pity. Ah'm happy. What is it that makes you, an' my old woman and the council, want ter stop me keeping birds? What is it?"

Not being used to emotion which he can't control, the Rev. moves away a bit.

"No, dinna gan away," sez Geordie. "This little cree is the hall of democracy."

The Rev. turns irresolutely.

"Cum on, say yer say," sez Geordie. "Dinna tell me that you're ganna turn tail the first time somebody contradicts yer."

The Rev. coughs. "I will only say that this shed is an eyesore to the neighbourhood, to the council, and an irritation to your wife."

"The neighbours niver think about me an' me cree; they've got plenty ter bother their heads about. The council's an eyesore to me, so that's tit fer tat. And as fer being an irritation to my wife — well, iverything's an irritation to her, including hersel'! That leaves only the Lord God. If it's a sin against Him, why doesn't He tell me Hisself instead of sending a lackey?"

"God has vouchsafed His truth to His ministers," sez the Reverend.

"Ah dinna believe that," sez Geordie. "Arl men are equal, and God's truth belangs ter me as well as to you. You've got no monopoly of truth."

The Rev. looks hastily at his watch.

"Er — well, Mr Howell, I've got a Sisterhood meeting this afternoon. Think over what I've said, won't you?"

"Ah'll try," said Geordie, winking at the parson's white lie. The Rev. blushes.

"Good morning, Mr Howell."

"So long, Mr Jefferies. You'll think over what *Ah've* said, won't you?"

"Certainly," sez the Rev. "Most certainly," willing to say anything as long as he gets away.

So he walks away, feeling a bit puzzled and angry. But by the time that he's out of the allotment and passing Geordie's house he's quite normal again, so he calls in and talks to Mrs Howell for a while.

"Ah, Mrs Howell," he sez. "Your poor husband is fixed in the ways of sin. The devil has him snared. Let us watch and pray."

"Amen!" sez Mrs Howell, tightening her lips. Having snared Geordie forty years ago, she thinks it is a reflection upon her that the devil should take her prey.

And John Willy is writing a ten-thousand-word report out for the council, with a volume of Hansard at one elbow and Webster's at the other.

WHICH ENGLISH?

Now when John Willy reports this unexpected bit of defiance at the next council meeting, sparing nothing and adding a good bit, there's a lot of steam let off and everybody makes speeches. And the new Tories is worse than the old, for they make the most spitting and spluttering about the dignity of the council. So they instructs the clerk to get the bummers into action, instantly. And John Willy rubs his hands and sleeps well in his bow-windowed villa that night. Let him sleep.

The next day, when Geordie goes up t' hill to feed his pigeons what should he see but John Willy and a gang of hefty fellers engaged in tearing down his beloved cree while the pigeons fly around in great dismay, for they think that this is the end of the old homestead, and Geordie must have left them in the lurch.

"Hey!" shouts Geordie. "Yer can't do that!" including many unprintables in his excitement, of course.

John Willy smirks in the most infuriating manner and waves a document in the air. "This sez I can," he squeaks.

"Let me see that," sez Geordie.

"You can't read," sez this little sourpuss.

"Read!" sez Geordie. "Read! Why, yer little whippersnapper, I was reading when you was a twinkle in yer father's eye — whoever yer father was. Gimme that paper."

So John Willy hands him the paper. Geordie reads it and realises that the law is on the side of John Willy and the councillors.

But is he downcast? No fear! Our Geordie has plenty up his sleeve yet. He therefore salvages his big wickerwork baskets from the ruins of the old cree and calls his birds. One by one they flutter down. He shouts to some bairns playing nearby, and they help him with the baskets. But before he goes he has one last shot.

"John Willy," he sez, "gan back and tell them little Muzzos and Hitlers that you've pulled the auld man's cree down, but he's not beat yet. Ask them if they'll pull a council house down, 'cos that's where Ah'm ganning ter keep them birds of mine. And leave them boards; they'll make a decent bit of firewood, anyway."

And away he goes. His intention is to keep the birds in his back yard and give them the run of the house, but he's reckoned without the missis. She's waiting for him at the yard gate, and she gets the first word in.

"You're not bringing any of them stinkin', useless birds into my house," she sez.

"Oh," sez Geordie. "Your house! Always thought it was me that brought the money in."

"Thought!" she shouts. "Thought! That's what you've always done. Well, ter-day you've thought wrong. You're not bringin' them birds in here, so that's that!"

WHICH ENGLISH?

Geordie grins, and sez quietly, "So long, Hetty."

And away he marches with his wickerwork baskets. She sees that she's gone too far this time, and cries out, frightened like: "George, George, where yer gannin'?" But there is no answer. The worm has turned.

Now, opposite the council chambers there is a bit of waste ground. Pretty soon all kinds of rumours begin to go the rounds. Lorries pull up and begin to deposit brickets and timber. Foundations are laid. Some say that it's going to be a new picture house; others that it's a new grocery shop. A few whisper tales about Geordie Howell, him that's separated from his wife, talking to the foreman, and the foreman laughing his head off fit to kill, and bandy-legged little Geordie grinning all over his face. But nobody guesses that the new place is being built for Geordie, which it is, for Geordie has a nice little nest-egg saved, and he figures he'll build himself a new home of his own with it, which is sensible.

And when this house is built there's hell to pay in the council-chamber. For this new house has a balcony on the second floor where the pigeons walk up and down before entering through the little trapdoors which Geordie has so kindly provided for them. And every time there's a council meeting our Geordie steps out on to the balcony and whistles his birds home. And home they come, heedless of the fuming councillors – stragglers, tumblers, tamed wild 'uns and straight racing birds with blue blood in their veins, swooping from the blue, passing, on their way to the balcony, a garden gate upon which is proudly inscribed:

Sid Chaplin

Suggested activities

1
a What did you think of the story?
b What is supposed to be wrong with what Geordie is doing?
c Give your reasons for being on Geordie's side or against him.

2 In lines 1-20 the author introduces us to the main character and sets the scene.

a What do you learn about Geordie from these lines?
b Why do you think that the author contrasts the importance of the pigeon cree to Geordie with what he does for a living? You might find it helpful to look at lines 55–65.

WHICH ENGLISH?

3 Explain what you think is meant or suggested by the following:

a and not caring how soon it's here either (*line 9*)
b Hated it from the first day he dropped into the blackness (*line 11*)
c which is a pretty important job in his estimation (*lines 24–25*)
d the puffings an' blowings of a sourpuss of a council clerk (*line 28*)
e in a local-authority tone of voice (*line 29*)
f Men, like creeping things and dumb beasts, are drawn outside by the sun (*lines 67–8*)
g he's a hardened case and the devil's got his talons deep (*line 76*)
h Not being used to emotion which he can't control (*line 117*)
i – well, iverything's an irritation to her, including hersel'! (*lines 128–9*)
j winking at the parson's white lie (*line 137*)
k Having snared Geordie forty years ago (*line 148-9*)
l The worm has turned (*line 199*)

4

a Describe your impression from this story of what Geordie's wife looks like and how she behaves.

b Make up a conversation between:

   either
   Geordie and his wife discussing the pigeon cree

   or
   Geordie's wife and the clergyman when she goes to visit him.

   You may find it helpful to do this with a partner and to tape-record the conversation.

5 From lines 21–33 pick out any words or phrases that give you a clear impression of the clerk from the council who has come to visit Geordie.

6 The clerk is named John William Thwaites and the clergyman is referred to as the Reverend James Aloysis Jefferies.

a Do these names themselves suggest anything to you about the people?

b Discuss with a friend how far you are influenced by the sound of a person's name before you meet them.

c Make up your own names for the following imaginary people, using names which suggest something of the quality listed.

   a houseproud person
   a quick-tempered person
   someone who is too good to be true
   someone who is sly and cunning

WHICH ENGLISH?

d The novelist, Charles Dickens, often gave his characters names that suggested something about them and how they behaved. Here are just six of the names Dickens used. What do the names suggest to you about the person so named?

Mr M'Choakumchild, a schoolmaster
Mr Bounderby, a banker and factory owner
Mr Veneering
Lady Dedlock
Uriah Heep
Esther Summerson

7 'Geordie' is the nick-name of the man in the story. What is his real name?

8 'Geordie' is a term used of a man or woman who comes from a particular area of the British Isles and who speaks in a distinctive way. Find out to which area the term refers and write down names of any well-known Geordies you have heard of.

9 Several different names are used to describe people who come from a particular area and who speak in a distinctive way. Here are some well-known examples. Find out which area is referred to in each case and consider the reasons why these names are used.

Cockney,
Brummie,
Jock,
Taffy,
Yorkie,
Scouse,
Paddy.

Sometimes the names are used as a compliment and sometimes as a deliberate insult. Discuss reasons why people might be offended or pleased at being called by one of these names, or by a similar one that you can think of. Would *you* like to have a nick-name which referred to the area you came from or the way you speak?

10 A **'dialect'** is a form of speech which is used in a particular district. The way most of us speak reflects the region in which we were brought up. We pronounce words differently from people who live in other parts of the country, and sometimes we use words to mean different things. In some areas, for example, you might find people referring to 'bairns' instead of children, or saying that they were going to 'brew a cup of tea' or 'mash tea' when they were going to make a cup of tea.

WHICH ENGLISH?

Standard English is the term used to describe the dialect of English which is usually used in printed materials, and taught in schools. Although it is a particular dialect, Standard English is spoken with a variety of accents.

Received Pronunciation refers to that accent of English which does not vary from region to region. It is, for example, the accent used in BBC news bulletins.

In the story, 'The Pigeon Cree', the author tries to suggest the way in which the dialect of Geordie differs from that of the clerk and clergyman. Make a list of some of the dialect differences that appear. Can you understand them all? Why do you think the clergyman speaks a different dialect of English?

A dialect has phrases and sayings that are only used in a particular area. 'Ah'm not as green as Ah'm cabbage-looking' (*lines 111–12*) might be one of these. If you lived near Leeds you might understand:

'Ee's lakin at taws up a ginnel' = He is playing marbles in the alleyway.

If you lived in the Black Country (an area just north of Birmingham) you might understand:

'Ther cat ran up our entry' = That person is a distant relation of mine.

The following definitions are taken from a humorous guide to Australian English – *Let Stalk Strine* – compiled by Afferbeck Lauder. In order to work out the meaning, you will have to read each phrase or sentence aloud using Received Pronunciation. It will help to work with a partner. When you have discovered the meanings try using a similar spelling system to transcribe another dialect which you know well.

> **Ear's Eve:** The festive occasion of 31st December. Each year, at midnight, Strines throughout the land perform the ceremony of joining hands with strangers and chanting 'Shoulder Quaint's Beef Cot' (also known as 'Frolang Zine').
>
> **Ebb Tide:** Hunger; desire for food. As in: 'I jess dono watser matter, Norm, I jess got no ebb tide these dyes.'
>
> **Egg Jelly:** In fact; really. As in: 'Well, there's nothing egg jelly the matter with her. It's jess psychological.'
>
> **Egg Nishner:** A mechanical device for cooling and purifying the air of a room.
>
> **Garbler Mince:** Within the next half hour. Also Greetings. As in: 'I'll be with you in a garbler mince', or 'With the garbler mince of the Gem of Directors.'
>
> **Gloria Soame:** A spurban house of more than fourteen squares, containing fridge, telly, wart wall carps, payshow, and a kiddies' rumps rooms. Antonym: Terror Souse.

WHICH ENGLISH?

> **Harps:** Thirty minutes past the hour. As: Harps two; harps four; harps tail; etc. Related words are: Fipes; temps; corpse. As: Fipes one; temps two; corpse four.
>
> **Jess Tefter; Lefter:** It is necessary to. As in: 'She'll jess tefter get chews twit', or 'You lefter filner form.'
>
> **Laze and Gem:** Usual beginning of a public speech. Often combined with Miss Gem. As in: 'Miss gem, laze and gem. It gives me grape leisure . . .
>
> **Mare Chick:** Effects produced by the assistance of supernatural powers. As: Bleck mare chick; mare chick momence; 'Laugh, your mare chick spell is airfree ware.'
>
> **Panam:** Unit of weight. As: A panam inn smeat.
>
> **Scared Saul:** Mythical hero. Believed to have been the originator and spiritual head of the Boy Scat movement. This movement, so popular with Strines and New Strines alike, embraces also the Gurgides, Sea Scats, Brannies and Carbs. Scared Saul (known to his intimates as Jobber Bob) is thought to have been in some way related to Gloria Sara Titch.
> The meeting place and local centre of Scat activity is known everywhere today as the Scared Saul.
>
> **Semmitch:** Two slices of bread with a filling in between, e.g. M-semmitch; semmon semmitch; chee semmitch. When ordering semmitches the following responses are indicated:
> A: Sell semmitches?
> B: Air, emeny jiwant?
> A: Gimmie utter martyr and an airman pickle. Emma chisit? (or Emma charthay?)
>
> **Would never:** Do not have. As in: 'You would never light wood-germite?' or 'Ar would never glue.'

11 Make a list of any sayings or phrases which are distinctive of the area in which you live. Explain what they mean. You might like to compile a short 'Guide' or 'Phrase Book' to be used by visitors to your area. This should give a clear idea of what is said and how it is pronounced.

12 You have listed phrases, and also tried to read 'sayings' which are distinctive of certain areas. The writers of the following poems have put a story into *their* dialect forms. Try to read them aloud. The overall sense is clear, although you may have to guess the meaning of one or two of the words.

  Discuss the use of traditional stories and themes and decide whether or not the subject matter suits the treatment it has received.

  Would the second poem be as effective if it were written in Standard English?

WHICH ENGLISH?

A Black Country Carol

It 'appened many 'ear agone,
As yo ull all recall:
A babby naime o' Jesus Christ
Was born t' save us all.
'Is faither was a werkin' mon,   5
Jo 'ad no claim to faime;
'Is mother 'er was only a wench,
And Mary was 'er naime.

They 'ad ter goo ter Bethlehem
On account o' the guverment.   10
But the plaice was welly packed wi' folk,
And there wor no room ter rent.
Now Mary 'er was clemmed ter jeth
And the babby was redy ter come;
So they shook down wi' th'osses and cows,   15
'Cos they couldn't find e'er a wum.

The babby come at jed o' night
Wi'out trial or mishap.
The parents 'earts were fit to bust
Wi' pride at the little chap.   20
The angels they wun mekin' a din
As the star shone overhead,
When shepherds and a two-three kings
Come wanderin' to the shed.

They gid the babby gifts o' go'd   25
And other expensive stuff.
Now werkin' men cor do the saime
'Cos we doa earn enough.
But we con werk wi' honest 'ond
And sweat wi' all we might   30
And so mek all Black Country folk
Dacent in 'is sight

Mary Chitham

T' Cure

Owld Widder Waites sat up i' bed,
A sorry-lookin' bein',
An' to her only son, she said,
"John Bill, I think I'm deein'."

"Who's bahn to wesh an' cook for thee, 5
An', mend thi socks an' clo'es?
Who can there be in t' place o' me?"
She sobbed, an' blew her nose.

"I think tha'd better find thisen
A wife, to tak' mi place; 10
— A nice, hard-workin' lass, an' then
I'll leave thee wi' good grace."

"Nay, mother, nay!" cried young John Bill,
"Tha munnot go an' dee!
There isn't a lass this side o' th' hill 15
Can cook as good as thee!"

"It's no use talkin'," she replied,
"Tha knows I'm not so clivver;
Tha needs another at thi side,
— We dunnot last for ivver." 20

Na, t' lad were sweet on Sally Kaye,
A dizzy little dolly,
Wi' big blue een, an' hair like hay,
— As brainless as a brolly.

An' when he browt her home next day, 25
To show her to his mother,
Th' owld lass recovered straight away,
An' baht' a bit o' bother.

"Good Lord!" she cried, till t' rafters shook
Wi' t' force of her thanksgivin'- 30
"It's all reight, Sally; tak' thi hook;
I'd better go on livin'!"

William Beaumont

WHICH ENGLISH?

Further activities

13 Working with a partner, choose a topic which can be made into a piece of dialect writing. You may wish to select a recognisable story such as that in 'The Black Country Carol', or a humorous incident as in 'T' Cure'. One of the sayings which you listed in answer to question 11 could give you a title and an idea. If you are unable to tackle a complete story, try to write out a dialect conversation between people at a bus stop, or between neighbours gossiping. (See page 44 for notes on setting down conversation in writing.)

14 Prepare a speech for a debate or write an essay on the subject of

either
Dialects are a bad thing because they make it difficult for people of the same country to understand each other.

or
We should try to preserve our dialects because they are colourful and expressive and add to the interest and variety of a language.

15 Write an amusing story in which you get the better of authority. Remember to set the scene and introduce yourself as the main character carefully. Try to let the amusement of the situation arise out of what happens.

8
REAL LIFE DRAMA

The article printed below appeared in 'The Observer' newspaper on 8 August 1982. In it, Sir Ranulph Fiennes describes the end of the expedition that he led round the world from the North Pole to the South Pole and back to the North Pole around the other side of the world. He tells how he and his companion completed the last stage of their expedition which had lasted for three years. The picture on page 77 was taken as the two men were a short distance from the completion of their journey.

TRANSGLOBE: Three years with fear of failure

SIR RANULPH FIENNES, leader of the Transglobe Expedition, files an exclusive despatch from the Arctic Ocean on his long-awaited rendezvous with his ship after 99 days waiting on an ice-floe.

It was early in the evening when we first spotted the twin masts of our ship above the horizon of ice boulders, the ship that had for so long been our floating home, her volunteer crew like a close family to us.

A year before she had dropped us off at the mouth of the Yukon River. Seeing her again at the end of a three-year struggle, of three years of mental anguish caused by the fear of failure, I felt a surge of wild emotion. I don't think I shall ever forget the feeling of that wonderful moment.

The next few miles took eight and a half hours to traverse, and involved some hair-raising moments. But so what? At this point we felt nothing could stop us reaching our ship, our faithful friend and a safe, solid refuge, after the long, long months afloat on the fragile and unpredictable skin of the Arctic Ocean.

The sea ice of the Arctic is an awful

place to spend a summer holiday unless you are exceedingly jaded with life.

But after Charlie Burton and I had travelled a mere 300 miles south from the North Pole on our snowmobiles I decided to stop as soon as we could find a reasonably solid-looking floe, pitch camp and start floating.

Strong winds and rising temperatures were breaking up the ice. Our snowmobiles and sleds broke through the ice crust with disturbing frequency and we had several close escapes.

It was now painfully apparent to me that we were not going to make the latitude of Spitzbergen, or anywhere near it, before the sea ice broke up.

Most of our advisers in England and even Charlie felt that we should try to continue much further south under our own steam. While respecting that view, I instinctively felt the need for caution. Whichever decision I made might end in failure, and I would have no one to blame but myself.

The outcome of starting to 'float' too soon and from too far north might be to end up well short of the ice edge when summer ended and new ice formed in August/September 1982; a rendezvous with our boat would then be out of the question.

On the other hand, to risk continued travel over rapidly deteriorating ice might lead to any one of several irretrievable situations.

At about 86 degrees north we stopped on a solid-looking floe. It was 25 April. I had planned to travel until early June, so the disappointment was considerable. We were to camp for 99 days on our drifting floe. During all that period we had no bad feelings and the atmosphere between us was harmonious.

This was in no way attributable to saintly characters, since we are both opinionated, sensitive and quick-tempered. It was rather the result of many years working together in close proximity and unpleasant environments.

What did we do with ourselves? Very little. We just went into a sort of trance.

Since the tents were cramped, we could not stand up. The 'floors' of axed ice were uneven and daily became more sodden with melt water, making sitting down impracticable. So we lay in our sleeping bags to keep out the damp and cold. We never washed as there was no point.

When polar bears visited the tent we scrambled into boots, jackets and trousers, grabbed guns and cautiously unzipped tent flaps, to view our massive co-drifters. Carefully placed shots would usually scare them away at a slow proud amble, seldom at a run.

In all, 18 bears came to our camp. We photographed and filmed one large adult from four yards away as it strode over the guy ropes at the other end of a little tent, licking its lips with a long, black tongue.

These were all big events in our daily existence. At noon I took a sunshot with a theodolite to find out where we were drifting. Twice a day, when ionospheric conditions allowed, I radioed Ginnie, my wife, saying where and how we were. She looked after our main radio base at faraway Cape Nord, in Greenland.

By the end of July our ship, the MV *Benjamin Bowring*, had twice turned back to Spitzbergen after vain attempts to penetrate the pack ice to the south of us.

The governor of Spitzbergen had expressed concern about our safety and lack of time that remained this summer. Two of our sponsors and London committee members had flown over the ice and reported back in warning terms.

I was therefore advised to abandon our drift while there was still a chance of rescue by aircraft. It was pointed out, quite rightly, that if I failed to take this chance all responsibility for any resulting search and rescue attempt would be mine alone.

All the ship's crew, the main body of our expedition, supported a continued attempt at a rendezvous despite their previous abortive attempt. And so for a third time our 30 year old vessel set out, and despite omnipresent fogbanks managed with great perseverance and considerable nerve to batter their way to within 10 miles of our floe.

By last Monday it was clear that they could get no closer, so despite the highly unstable and often rotten ice between us, we decided to risk a dash across the last gap as soon as there was a lift in the usual low fog.

The next afternoon, at 13.30 Greenwich Time, the weather was clear and windy. With safety kit and food for 10 days our canoe/sledges weighed 400 lb each.

After a few hundred yards each of us broke a ski tip and progress was painfully slow. At one stage we progressed only 200 yards in one hour, and Charlie told me he felt sick and exhausted.

Since our ski attachments were broken we knocked them off with Charlie's axe and thereafter dragged the naked canoes straight over the rough, broken ice on their thin hulls.

Whenever we came to pools, rivers and lakes of whipped water, we gingerly pulled the boats off the rotten ice banks and tried to get in them before the edge broke off. Balance was a problem. So was the cold wind, especially as our feet and hands were soon wet and numb.

But once aboard the *Bowring* all that was forgotten. I was luckier than Charlie, for among the deckful of smiling faces, quiet and very blue-eyed, was Ginnie. Only when she was firmly in my somewhat rank embrace did the full realisation sink in.

We had completed, at last, our impossible dream.

Sir Ranulph Fiennes

Suggested activities

1. This report was written for a newspaper by Sir Ranulph Fiennes. Discuss with a partner whether or not you find it interesting, and pick out the phrases which you think give the sense of a difficult journey that took three years to complete.

2. The author would probably have described his experiences in a different way to his wife, Ginnie. It is also possible that his friend Charlie would not have seen what happened in the same way as the author. Consider these possibilities and then:

REAL LIFE DRAMAS

either
Write an imaginary conversation over the radio which the author could have had with Ginnie. (If you cannot remember how to set out conversation in writing, look at the notes on page 44.)

or
Write one or two paragraphs about the journey from Charlie Burton's point of view.

3 Working on your own or with a partner, pick out at least one phrase or group of words which seems to show the following:

a the appearance of the surface of the sea
b the close relationship between all members of the expedition
c a feeling of sudden excitement
d the writer's sense of being responsible for what happened
e that the writer may have had a sense of humour.

4 The writer of this article gives you a brief idea of what he experienced and felt during the last ten miles of his journey. Imagine that you have been away on an expedition for three years and that rescue is only ten miles away.

either
Write about what happens to you and what your thoughts and emotions are as you see the first sign of your rescue vessel on the horizon.

or
Improvise, with two or three friends, the events of those last ten miles. You are exhausted, low on rations and possibly in danger. Difficult areas of ice, jungle, mountain or water may have to be crossed before you are safe. What are your reactions and what happens? What do you say to each other?

5 There are many famous stories about people trying to overcome Nature or exploring the unknown. Imagine you are one of them and describe your thoughts and feelings as you *begin* your journey. Here are some suggestions, but you may choose your own subject if you wish. (Notice that some of these explorers were alone; others had a number of companions).

a Captain Scott setting off for the Antarctic.
b Amy Johnson about to fly to Australia.
c Neil Armstrong preparing for the first journey to the moon.
d Clare Francis about to sail round the world.

6 'We had completed, at last, our impossible dream.'
   Describe a real or imaginary experience when you finally achieved what you had set out to do. It may be something very small, but it should be something that required determination and persistence.

REAL LIFE DRAMAS

7 Prepare and, if possible, give a short speech entitled: 'Climbing mountains or rowing the Atlantic is a waste of time and money'. You may argue for or against the motion.
   (You may find the guidance on 'putting a case' on page 142 helpful to you.)

8 Read the following short account called 'The Castaway', in which a man, close to desperation, hopes that he will be rescued from his raft. When you have read it, discuss your reactions with a partner and, together, try to make up a convincing explanation of the events or to continue the story.

THE CASTAWAY

The man on the raft had only hope to keep him alive now. The bones showed through his thin face. An endless moan escaped his trembling mouth. His eyes were bright with fever. He had been clinging to life for more than a month now on this wretched collection of planks.

All at once a new sound reached his enfeebled brain; a buzzing noise imagined in his delirium no doubt. But it wasn't – it really was a helicopter approaching slowly, flying over the raft. Saved! He was saved! The castaway danced about clumsily.

In the meantime a rope-ladder had been lowered from the helicopter. A man dressed in rags, his emaciated face overgrown with a coarse beard, was pushed brutally on to the top rungs.

The helicopter turned away and disappeared.

Now there were two castaways on the raft.

Rolan Topor

Further activities

9 Choose three or four people from the class to act as a panel of judges. Read or show to them the work done in answering question 8 and ask them to decide which explanation or continuation of the story is the most convincing. They must give full reasons for their choice which they must be prepared to defend.

10 Imagine you are going on a difficult and possibly dangerous expedition. In a group decide what small additional items (compass, strong thread, etc.) you will take in case of emergency. The items will have to fit into a small biscuit tin because that is all you have room for.

REAL LIFE DRAMAS

■ ■ The following true story recounts how a girl survived a plane crash in the jungle. Could you have done the same?

SHE LIVED AND 91 OTHERS DIED

Haggard, bruised, still dazed, 17-year-old Juliane Koepcke gazed out of the light plane carrying her back to civilization from an incredible ordeal in the Peruvian wilds. Far below, scattered in the treetops and over the floor of the jungle, lay the bits and pieces of the airliner that Juliane had been riding in when it broke apart in mid-air and crashed. And hidden in the jungle were the broken bodies of her 91 fellow passengers. Almost miraculously, Juliane had been spared. Somehow, this delicate, almost frail-looking girl had not only survived the long fall from the plane, but had managed, for nine days, to stay alive in the wilderness.

Juliane's odyssey started with joyful anticipation. She had just graduated from high school in Lima, the capital, and now was going home for Christmas to her parents' remote home in the jungle. About 5 feet 5 inches and weighing barely 100 pounds, she was the only child of two German-born scientists: animal ecologist Hans Koepcke and his ornithologist wife, Marie.

Juliane, her mother and a cheerful Christmas Eve crowd boarded the Lockheed Electra for the hour-and-half flight to the jungle town of Pucallpa. The plane climbed over the towering grey Andes and began its long descent into the flat, green Amazon valley below. There was no sign of trouble when the pilot instructed the passengers to fasten their seat-belts for the landing at Pucallpa.

Suddenly, the Electra was sledge-hammered by a violent jungle storm. Juliane saw a searing, lightning-like flash. Flames tore over the right wing. Alarmed, she looked at her mother, who said: 'This is the end of everything.' That was the last Juliane saw of her.

REAL LIFE DRAMAS

The next moment, Juliane felt as if she was being blown through the air. Strapped in her seat, she felt herself twisting, whirling, falling.

Juliane first heard the jungle birds. A canopy of green trees screened the late afternoon sunlight from above. About three hours had passed. She was lying on the jungle floor, still in her airplane seat. The two seats next to her were empty. There seemed to be no other people around. She called, but no one answered. There was a pain in her right shoulder — her collar-bone was fractured — and a cut on her upper right arm. Besides these and some bruises and scratches, she seemed otherwise unhurt.

Though probably suffering from shock, she never lost her wits or the confidence that she would be found. She had spent much of her childhood in the jungle with her parents and she remembered that her father had taught her to walk downhill to find water and then to follow the water downstream. Eventually, he had said, as the stream becomes bigger, one is bound to find civilization.

She began pushing through the thick underbrush. The rain had turned the ground into a muddy swamp and her high-heeled shoes sank in. The underbrush ripped at her dress. After a while, she lost one shoe and stumbled on for a day with one bare foot. Then she lost the other.

During the first three days after the crash, Juliane heard planes and helicopters searching above her for survivors, but they could not see her through the dense growth of jungle trees.

On Sunday, two days after the crash, she reached a narrow *quebrada*, or riverbed, at the headwaters of the Sheboya River and began to follow it. In many places she found it easier to swim along with the current than to walk. Her bare feet became black and blue; in some areas the ground was covered with thorns.

After the first three days, rain fell continually, and she was always wet. At night, shivering under trees, she slept only intermittently. She tried unsuccessfully to start a fire with her watch crystal. Insects and leeches bit her and her bites and cuts became infested with wormy larvae laid by flies. She saw few wild animals; some small crocodiles slithered off the shore after her in curiosity.

She ate nothing. She considered trying to catch some frogs, but was not sure which ones were poisonous. She picked some fruit and licked it hungrily but, again, she dared not eat it lest it be poisonous.

Four days after the crash, Juliane reached a small, thatched lean-to on the bank of the river. She had covered about ten air miles, but far more along her winding river course. Too weak to go any farther, she dragged herself inside and found some kerosene and salt.

After five days in the lean-to — nine days after the plane crashed — three hunters came by in a canoe. Struggling to the river bank, she waved and attracted their attention. The superstitious jungle men drew back, certain

REAL LIFE DRAMAS

that the blond girl was some sort of evil spirit, but eventually they came ashore and gave her sugar, salt and some *fariña* meal. With gasoline, they helped her clean more worms out of her skin.

The next morning, two more hunters appeared and took Juliane in their canoe to the hut of a native woman for further help. When the woman saw the red of Juliane's bloodshot eyes, she screamed 'Demon!' and tried to chase them away.

The hunters then took Juliane to the small settlement of Tournavista. There, a doctor treated her cuts and bruises and bandaged her. The following day, 11 days after the crash, an American woman pilot, Jerri Cobb, flew into the jungle airstrip and took Juliane to a camp of American missionaries at Yarinacocha, near Pucallpa, where she was reunited with her father.

Robert G. Hummerstone

Further activities

12 If this story were to be filmed or televised, how would you arrange it? What descriptions or incidents would you emphasise and why? In what order would you put the events of the story?

Working in small groups, discuss your ideas and make an outline plan for the film. You need not write down every conversation, but select details of scene, appearance, mood, which you would like to convey, and decide how you could show them.

You might, for example, think that a commentator would be necessary, or that the actress playing Juliane would give all the information about herself and her ordeal through her spoken thoughts.

You might proceed by noting down such things as the following.

a How many scenes will there be?
b Which actors/actresses will be needed in each scene?
c What scenes in the story, if any, could you miss out in making a film?
d Would you use the technique of 'flashbacks'?
e What props would be necessary?

You will also have to decide whether everything will be in English, or whether you will use the languages that were probably spoken.

13 Still working in your groups, try to write the film script. Remember this involves writing instructions for the camera crew as well as writing the dialogue. See page 44 for notes on setting out dialogue.

You might like to do this with another story included in this book. (The story of 'The Plague at Eyam' in Unit 2 might be suitable.)

9
APPROVING AND DISAPPROVING

The following extract is taken from a book called 'The Soccer Tribe' by Desmond Morris. It is not really about football, but about how people behave, especially when they are part of a group. In the passage, the writer compares what happens at a football match to the behaviour of a primitive tribe with its gods and its temples, its rituals and superstitions. Use a dictionary to help you with unfamiliar words.

SOCCER TRIBE

Every visit to a soccer match is a rich encounter with all its many tribal aspects at once. There, inevitably, are the harassed managers yelling tactical advice in their desperate hunt for goals; there, the triumphant players leaping to hug and embrace one another after a successful attack on the enemy; there, the elderly directors fussing over their League tables and dreaming of the status boost of promotion to a higher division; there, the choir-like chanting of the massed supporters as their idols reappear on the sacred turf; there, the muttering experts who have seen it all before and know with deep pessimism that the good old days of true sportsmanship are gone for ever; and there, the thinly clad young fans clustered on the icy terraces in a display of manliness, ready to cheer themselves hoarse for the soccer stars that they themselves can never be; the Soccer Tribe in all its curiously isolated and yet intensely public glory.

At the heart of each Soccer Tribe lies its great temple, the stadium. So strong is its magic that, for a tribesman to approach it, even on a day when no match is being played, creates a strange feeling of mounting excitement and anticipation. Although it is deserted he can sense the buzz of the crowd and hear again the roar of the fans as the ball hits the back of the enemy net. To a devoted tribesman it is a holy place, with a significance that it is hard for an outsider to appreciate.

APPROVING AND DISAPPROVING

Soaring into the sky at the four corners of the stadium are the huge tribal totem poles, the floodlight pylons. Sometimes these are gracefully tapering concrete pillars, but more often than not they are open metalwork towers, looking like oil-field derricks surmounted by batteries of powerful lamps. Rising high above the surrounding buildings, they are visible for great distances, a constant reminder of the hallowed ground that lies between them.

In the very centre of the Tribal Territory lies the sacred turf of the pitch itself, the green focus of all tribal activities. Known technically as 'the field of play', it is often referred to, by the players and managers, as 'the park'. What matters, they say, is what happens 'out on the park'. Like so many football words and phrases, this has an antique quality, dating back to the time when most matches were played on a marked-out section of public parklands, before the great crowds gathered to watch.

When they dress for the match, many of the tribesman take care not to forget the special mascot, charm, talisman or lucky garment they always carry to aid their team's success. They may treat their mascots almost as joke, but they would feel uneasy without them.

Later, as they head for the sacred ground and begin meeting their friends, there are repeated assurances that today they are bound to win, certain to massacre the enemy, sure, quite sure, to seem them utterly defeated. Anyone foolish enough to suggest the opposite is quickly silenced, for this is the time when tribal sorcery begins to take a grip. Even to speak of the possibility of losing might bring bad luck. The gods would be angry at such disloyalty.

Guided carefully into its special place in the car-park, the visiting team's coach comes to a halt. As the door hisses open, the tension already felt by the visiting players becomes acute. The back-chat and card-playing of the long trip are forgotten. As they walk briskly to the visitors' dressing room they may encounter members of the host team arriving from their homes nearby, but the two sides studiously ignore one another. There is virtually no contact between the opponents before the game, because of an unspoken feeling that to communicate would somehow give the other side an advantage.

Now the supporters are pouring into the ground and filling the stands, already starting up the tribal chants. The loudspeakers are blaring out pop music and the season-ticket holders are taking their familiar routes to their favourite seats, checking the team-lists in their programmes. The directors are assembling in the board-room for their hospitality rituals and the reporters and commentators are fortifying themselves with a last drink in one of the bars before mounting to the Press box. At the far end of the ground, the visiting supporters are being herded like wild horses into the special pen allocated to them, watched warily by the police who are trying to assess the likelihood of crowd trouble after the match. Deep inside the

APPROVING AND DISAPPROVING

grandstand the referee and his linesmen are changing into their sinister black costumes, as if in mourning for some unidentified death.

In the two dressing rooms, the players are preparing themselves for the struggle to come. Before the end of the afternoon several of them, at least, will have suffered severe cuts and bruises, perhaps even serious injury. Palms are already moist. Superstitious rituals are being faithfully carried out. The extroverts are making a fuss, joking nervously; the introverts are quietly withdrawn, concentrating exaggeratedly on little personal procedures that help to pass the time – bootlacing and bandaging, examining shinpads and studs, checking things that need no checking, doing muscle-exercises, jigging about. The smell of liniment hangs in the air. The manager makes his rounds, doling out words of advice and encouragement, as much to fill the vacuum of waiting as to provide last-minute instruction.

Suddenly, the sound the players have been waiting for like Pavlovian dogs abruptly fills the air – the referee's buzzer is summoning the teams on to the pitch. It sounds, too, in the board-room and the Tribal Elders pull on their overcoats and mount the stairs to their special seats. In the two dressing rooms, the buzzer triggers a dramatic change of mood. The players move about, shaking hands and wishing one another good luck. They begin to line up at their dressing room doors, the studs on their boots clattering on the hard floor as they exercise their legs, impatient to feel the turf beneath their feet, and the physical freedom of open space. Several are changing position in the group, trying to get themselves into the place that their private superstitions demand. Finally the door opens and the players advance, moving down the tunnel and out on to the expanse of the arena.

Desmond Morris

Suggested activities

1 Write down the following words and next to each of them write down another word or phrase which means the same thing. Try to choose words or phrases that will fit into the original sentence so that the meaning conveyed to the reader is the same.

harassed (*line 2*)
triumphant (*line 3*)
muttering (*line 8*)
devoted (*line 19*)
hallowed (*line 26*)
disloyalty (*line 44*)
familiar (*line 56*)

herded (*line 61*)
sinister (*line 64*)
superstitious (*line 69*)
extroverts (*line 70*)
introvert (*line 70*)
dramatic (*line 81*)

APPROVING AND DISAPPROVING

2 In your own words explain the following as carefully as you can:

a the choir-like chanting of the massed supporters as their idols re-appear on the sacred turf (*lines 7–8*)

b the thinly clad young fans clustered on the icy terraces in a display of manliness (*lines 10–11*)

c To a devoted tribesman it is a holy place (*line 19*)

d the tribesmen take care not to forget the special mascot, charm, talisman or lucky garment they always carry to aid their team's success (*lines 35–7*)

e The gods would be angry at such disloyalty (*line 44*)

f The directors are assembling in the board-room for their hospitality rituals (*lines 57–8*)

3 The writer makes several statements about soccer as a tribal ritual and then gives examples that illustrate these statements. In the first paragraph, for instance, he states that there are many different aspects of tribal behaviour to be seen at a soccer match, and then he comments on specific examples of that behaviour. Read the passage again and make brief notes in two columns headed 'General statements', and 'Examples illustrating these statements'.

4 The writer has discussed the tribal rituals of soccer in about 1,500 words. Using the column headed 'General statements' as a guide try to summarise the passage in about 150 words. Try to keep to the order used by the author, but leave out all the examples and any unnecessary descriptive words. The finished piece of work must 'flow' properly and contain all the important information.

5 Write an essay agreeing or disagreeing with Desmond Morris that football is a 'tribal activity' which is almost a religion. Plan your essay carefully; it will help you if you make a list of points and arrange them in a sensible order. You will need an introductory paragraph and, when you have finished presenting the different arguments 'for' and 'against', you will need a concluding paragraph expressing your final opinion. You should be able to extend the essay with observations drawn from your own experience. It is worth considering why football is an almost exclusively male pastime.

6 Prepare a speech which you would like to give in a class debate on the motion: 'The British are far too preoccupied with sport'.

APPROVING AND DISAPPROVING

7 Are there other activities (for example, rock music, package holidays, disco dancing, royal visits, weddings, cricket, riding motor cycles) in which people sometimes behave as if they were members of a tribal group, with objects of worship and special rituals? Describe an activity like this, either from the point of view of an outside observer like Desmond Morris or from the point of view of somebody who is totally committed.

The article which follows is an obituary written on the death of Bill Shankly, the famous manager of Liverpool Football Club. Bill Shankly could certainly be said to belong to the Soccer Tribe which Desmond Morris refers to, and the article itself gives you an idea of the sort of man he was and the importance he attached to football and to what happened to Liverpool FC. As you read the obituary decide whether the writer belongs to the Soccer Tribe.

Shanks for the Golden Memory

Opponents of Liverpool Football Club would be rash to assume that they have done with Bill Shankly. Once Bill's ashes have been scattered on the pitch at Anfield any visiting forward who is setting himself to score an important goal is liable to find suddenly that he has something in his eye.

Certainly Shanks would want us to believe in the possibility. Even after the results were in the paper, showing a scoreline against his men, he always refused to give defeat house-room. Maybe we should follow his example and regard his death as just an ugly rumour.

To those who knew him well his loss is about as sore as any could be. But there is some easing of the grief in the knowledge that few men ever had such a capacity for warming and delighting their fellows without being physically in their company. For many of us he really will always be there.

Most of the thousand and one Shankly anecdotes, the tales of his doings and utterances, are distorted and diminished in the telling but he communicated such a strong sense of himself that enough of what was unique and marvellous about him is bound to survive. Nearly everyone connected with British football has tried at one time or another to impersonate the accent and the mannerism he brought out of the south Ayrshire coalfield as a teenager and guarded against even the tiniest erosion through half a century in England. Few of the impersonators get within touching distance of the reality, but nobody minds. The Shankly legend is

APPROVING AND DISAPPROVING

the living, genuine article and the smallest fragment of it can spread laughter in any group of football people.

Clearly, however, he needed far more than earthy, utterly original wit to make the impact he did. His unshakable attachment to the ordinary supporters of football ('I'm a people's man – only the people matter') was a big help, but his real strength was, perhaps, drawn from something even more unusual.

With his drill-sergeant's hairstyle, his boxer's stance and his staccato, hard-man's delivery he did not fit everybody's idea of a romantic. But that's what he was, an out-and-out, 22-carat example of the species. His secret was that he sensed deep down that the only practical approach to sport is the romantic one. How else could a manager persuade grown men that they could find glory in a boys' game? Shankly did that and more.

Looking into the faces of some of his outstanding former players in the last few days, men like Ian St John and Ronnie Yeats and Kevin Keegan, we could see how much they felt they owed to the Boss. He gave them more than a share in trophies, nothing less than a wonderful dream.

He fed it into their spirits by many means, by humour, dedicated example and that romanticism that insisted on talking defeats away as if they were fleeting embarrassments that a malevolent and dishonest fate had inflicted on his teams without regard to their true worth. His performances in that line were like those of a witch doctor, full of blind faith and incantations. They worked so well that his players never allowed defeat to become a habit. Of course, he had learned plenty about the nuts and bolts of the game in his long career as a player with Carlisle, Preston (where he developed a bottomless admiration for Tommy – never Tom – Finney), and Scotland, and his management years at Carlisle, Grimsby, Workington, Huddersfield (where he had a brief memorable alliance with the young Denis Law) and from 1959 at Liverpool.

His Liverpool won the Second Division championship in 1962 by eight points and by the time he retired prematurely in 1974 they had taken the League title three times, the FA Cup twice and the UEFA Cup once. It is no diminution of the splendid manager who succeeded him, Bob Paisley, to say that Shankly left behind a foundation that contributed hugely to the subsequent domination of Europe by the club. He also left behind a great deal of himself and the pathos of his self-precipitated conversion into a peripheral, haunting, and sometimes embittered figure at Anfield was painful to his friends. But he was never reduced in the eyes of those who knew him best. No manager ever gave more to the spirit of a city or the folklore of a game than he did.

'Me having no education,' I once heard him say, 'I had to use my brains.' He used his heart, too. It was as big as a town.

Hugh McIlvanney

APPROVING AND DISAPPROVING

Further activities

8 What impression of Bill Shankly do *you* get from reading the passage? Write down at least three sentences which you think support your answer.

You will need to work with a partner in answering questions 9, 10, 11 and 12.

9 Discuss the sentences you have written down in answering question 8 with your partner. Explain to him/her why you chose those particular sentences. If she/he has written down different sentences, discuss those as well, and decide which give the clearest picture of the man.

10 When you have reached agreement with your partner, make *two* lists of what you have learned about Bill Shankly from reading the whole passage. The first list should contain facts (e.g. date and place of birth, when he died, where he was buried, details of his physical appearance). The second list should contain details of what you have learned about his personality and character (e.g. the writer says that 'he always refused to give defeat house-room' (*lines 6–7*), which suggests that Bill Shankly was a man of considerable determination who always expected his side to win).

11 How do you think Bill Shankly would have behaved before, during and after the match referred to in the extract from *The Soccer Tribe*? You may discuss this or write down what you think.

12 The writer of the article blends details of fact (your list 1) with his impressions of the man's character (your list 2), and manages to convey his own approval of Bill Shankly and his achievements.

a Discuss and then write down words or phrases which you think show that the writer liked and approved of Bill Shankly.

b Imagine that the newspaper had asked for an obituary from a writer who totally disapproved of football and the Soccer Tribe. Using exactly the same information as the author, re-write three sentences from the passage so that they suggest disapproval.

13 Think of someone you know, or invent an imaginary person, and make two lists about them and their personalities, as you did in question 10. Using *exactly* the same information in each paragraph, write one paragraph expressing dislike of the person and another showing approval of them.

For example, if someone does not spend money readily, you could show approval by saying that he/she is 'careful with his/her money' or that he/she is 'never extravagant'. The same person could be described as 'mean' or 'tight-fisted'. The fact remains the same, but the difference lies in your interpretation and description of it.

14 Choose a selection of daily newspapers in the local library and see if they print any obituaries. If someone well-known has died recently, their obituary will probably appear in several newspapers. Compare the information about that person given in the different versions, and decide what the writer thought of them, remembering of course that it would be unusual to say out-right something really bad about a person who has just died.

15 Choose a character from history whom you either admire or disapprove of, and write that person's obituary. To do this successfully you will need to

a make a list of the factual details about that person and
b make a list of the qualities of his/her personality and character.

When you arrange these details into an obituary, show your admiration or disapproval of the person about whom you have chosen to write. (You may find it helpful to refer back to any obituaries you found in answer to question 14, if any of them clearly indicate a point of view.)

16 You are one of six people in an air-borne balloon which is sinking towards the sea. To lighten the load so the balloon can reach its destination safely five of those people must be thrown overboard. Prepare a speech to give to the class explaining why you should be saved. You may speak as yourself, or pretend that you are any famous person, dead or alive.

When five other people have given their reasons for not being jettisoned, the remaining members of the class must vote on who should survive. The person who can give the most persuasive speech will evidently be left alive whilst the others go overboard!

10
RELATING TO OTHERS

The following story is set in Trinidad in the West Indies. It was written in 1928 and paints a picture of a way of life that is fast disappearing.

LA DIVINA PASTORA

Of my own belief in this story I shall say nothing. What I have done is to put it down as far as possible just as it was told to me, in my own style, but with no addition to or subtraction from the essential facts.

Anita Perez lived with her mother at Bande l'Est Road, just at the corner where North Trace joins the Main Road. She had one earthly aim. She considered it her duty to be married as quickly as possible, first because in that retired spot it marked the sweet perfection of a woman's existence, and secondly, because feminine youth and beauty, if they exist, fade early in the hard work on the cocoa plantations. Every morning of the week, Sunday excepted, she banded down her hair, and donned a skirt which reached to her knees, not with any pretensions to fashion but so that from seven till five she might pick cocoa, or cut cocoa, or dry cocoa or in some other way assist in the working of Mr Kayle Smith's cocoa estate. She did this for thirty cents a day, and did it uncomplainingly, because her mother and father had done it before her, and thriven on it. On Sundays she dressed herself in one of her few dresses, put on a little gold chain, her only ornament, and went to Mass. She had no thought of woman's rights, nor any Ibsenic theories of morality. All she knew was that it was her duty to get married, when, if she was lucky, this hard life in the cocoa would cease.

Every night for the past two years Sebastian Montagnio came down from his four-roomed mansion, half a mile up the trace, and spent about an hour, sometimes much more, with the Perez family. Always he sat on a bench by the door, rolling cheap cigarettes and half-hiding himself in smoke. He was not fair to outward view but yet Anita loved him. Frequently half an hour would elapse without a word from either, she knitting or sewing steadily, Sebastian watching her contentedly and Mrs Perez sitting on the ground just outside the door, smoking one of Sebastian's cigarettes and carrying on a ceaseless monologue in the local patois. Always when Sebastian left, the good woman rated Anita for not being kinder to him. Sebastian owned a few acres of cocoa and a large provision garden, and Mrs Perez had an idea that Anita's marriage would mean relief from the cocoa-work, not only for Anita but also for her.

Anita herself said nothing. She was not the talking kind. At much expense and trouble, Sebastian sent her a greeting card each Christmas. On them were beautiful words which Anita spelt through so often that she got to know them by heart. Otherwise, nothing passed between the two. That he loved no one else she was sure. It was a great consolation; but did he love her? Or was it only because his home was dull and lonely, and theirs was just at the corner that he came down every night?

As the months slipped by, Anita anxiously watched her naturally pale face in the little broken mirror. It was haggard and drawn with watching and waiting for Sebastian to speak. She was not young and her manner was not attractive. The gossiping neighbours looked upon her as Sebastian's property. Even in the little cocoa-house dances (Sebastian never went because he did not dance) she was left to herself most of the time. And then, she loved him.

It came about that Anita's aunt, who lived in Siparia, paid her a surprise visit one Sunday. She had not visited North Trace for years, and might never come back again. Consequently there were many things to be talked about. Also the good lady wanted to know what Anita was doing for herself.

'And when will you be married, ma chère?' she asked, secure in the possession of three children and a husband. Anita, aching for a confidante, poured fourth her simple troubles into the married lady's sympathetic ear. Mrs Perez expatiated on Sebastian's worldly goods. Mrs Reis, you remember, came from Siparia. 'Pack your clothes at once, girl,' she said, 'you will have to miss this week in the cocoa. But don't mind, I know someone who can help you. And that is La Divina.'

Of La Divina Pastora, the Siparia saint, many things can be written but here only this much need be said. It is a small image of some two feet in height which stands in the Roman Catholic Church at Siparia. To it go pilgrims from all parts of the island, at all times of the year: this one with an incurable malady, that one with a long succession of business misfortunes, the other with a private grudge against some fellow creature to be satisfied, some out of mere curiosity. Once a year there used to be a special festival, the Siparia fête, when, besides the worshippers, many hundreds of sight-seers and gamblers gathered at the little village, and for a week there were

RELATING TO OTHERS

wild Bacchanalian carouses going on side by side with the religious celebrations. This has been modifed but still the pilgrims go. To many, the saint is nothing more than a symbol of the divine. To more – like the Perez family – it possesses limitless powers of its own to help the importunate. From both parties it receives presents of all descriptions, money frequently, but ofttimes a gift from the suppliant – a gold ring perhaps, or a brooch, or some article of jewellery. Anita had no money; her aunt had to pay her passage. But she carried the little gold chain with her, the maiden's mite, for it was all that she had. It was not fête time, and quietly and by herself, with the quiet hum of the little country village in her ears, Anita placed the chain around the neck of the Saint and prayed – prayed for what perhaps every woman except Eve has prayed for, the love of the man she loved.

That Sunday night when Sebastian reached Madam Perez's house, the even tenor of his way sustained a rude shock. Anita was not there, she had gone to Siparia and was not coming back till next Sunday, by the last train. Wouldn't he come in and sit down? Sebastian came in and sat down on his old seat, near the door. Mrs Perez sat outside commenting on the high price of shop goods generally, especially tobacco. But Sebastian did not answer; he was experiencing new sensations. He missed Anita's quiet face, her steady nimble fingers, her glance at him and then away, whenever he spoke. He felt ill at ease, somehow disturbed, troubled, and it is probable that he recognised the cause of his trouble. For when Anita landed at Princes' Town the next Sunday, Tony the cabman came up to her and said: 'Sebastian told me to bring you up alone, Anita.' And he had to say it again before she could understand. During the six-mile drive, Anita sat in a corner of the cab, awed and expectant. Faith she had, but for this she was not prepared. It was too sudden, as if the Saint had had nothing to do with it.

They met Sebastian walking slowly down the road to meet them. For an hour he had been standing by her house, and as soon as the first cab passed, started, in his impatience to meet her on the way. The cab stopped and he was courageous enough to help her down. The cabman jumped down to light one of his lamps and the two stood waiting hand in hand. As he drove off Sebastian turned to her. 'Nita,' he said, shortening her name for the first time, 'I missed you, Nita. God how I missed you!'

Anita was happy, very happy indeed. In her new-found happiness she came near to forgetting the Saint, whose answer had come so quickly. Sebastian himself was very little changed. Still he came every night, still Mrs Perez smoked his cigarettes, ruminating now on her blissful future. But things were different. So different in fact that Sebastian proposed taking her to the little cocoa-house dance which was to come off in a day or two. It was the first time that they were going out together since that Sunday. Everybody who did not know before would know now, when they saw Sebastian taking her to the dance, a thing he had never done before. So she

RELATING TO OTHERS

dressed herself up with great care in the blue muslin dress, and what with happiness and excitement looked more beautiful than she had ever seen herself. Then, as she cast another look in the mirror she missed something. 'How I wish,' she said with a genuine note of regret in her voice, 'how I wish I had my little gold chain.' Here, her mother, determined not to jeopardise her future, called sharply to her, and she came out, radiant.

The dance continued till long after five o'clock, but Anita had to leave at three. Sebastian got tired of sitting down in a corner of the room while she whisked around. He felt just a trifle sulky, for he had wanted to leave an hour before, but she, drinking of an intoxicating mixture of admiration, success and excitement, had implored him to stay a little longer. They went home almost in silence, he sleepy, she tired, each thinking the other offended. It was the first little cloud between them.

'It is nothing,' thought Anita, 'we shall make it up tomorrow night.' She thought of something and smiled, but as she peeped at Sebastian and saw him peeping at her, she assumed a more serious expression. Tomorrow, not tonight.

Once inside the bedroom she started to undress quickly, took out a few pins and went to the table to put them down in the cigarette tin in which she kept her knick-knacks. Her mother, who was lying on the bed and listening with half-closed eyes to Anita's account of the dance, was startled by a sudden silence, followed by the sound of a heavy fall. She sprang down quickly, bent over the prostrate form of Anita, and turned to the little table to get the smelling-salts. Then she herself stood motionless, as if stricken, her senseless daughter lying unheeded on the floor. There in its old place in the cigarette tin, lay a little chain of gold.

C.L.R. James

Suggested activities

1 How do you think the necklace got back into the tin? Think carefully about the writer's account and make up your own explanation. If you find it difficult to make your explanation convincing you can suggest an alternative ending to the story. You should be able to justify your version of what happened.

2 In groups, discuss what you learn from the story about:

Anita Perez, Anita's mother, Sebastian Montagnio.

Write down brief notes under such headings as 'Where they live', 'What they do for a living', 'How they dress', 'How they speak' and so on.

RELATING TO OTHERS

3

a What was 'La Divina Pastora'?

b List the different reasons why people went to Siparia to visit the shrine.

4 What do you understand by the following phrases and sentences and what do they suggest to you about the people referred to?

a She had no thought of women's rights (*line 17*)

b He was not fair to outward view (*lines 23–4*)

c Anita's marriage would mean relief from the cocoa-work, not only for Anita but also for her (*lines 31–2*)

d The gossiping neighbours looked upon her as Sebastian's property (*lines 43–4*)

5

a What new sensations do you think Sebastian experiences when he visits Anita's home while she is away?

b Imagine that you are Sebastian and write a short description of your feelings (i) on learning that Anita has gone and (ii) when you know that she is due to return home.

In what ways will you behave differently from now on?

6 Perhaps the saint had answered Anita's prayer, but what other explanations can you think of that could account for the change in the relationship between Sebastian and Anita?

7 Find these words in the story and make sure that you understand their meanings. Use a dictionary if you need to.

pretensions (*line 11*)   supplicant (*line 72*)
monologue (*line 28*)   tenor (*line 80*)
consolation (*line 37*)   awed (*line 91*)
confidante (*line 52*)   ruminating (*line 104*)
malady (*line 62*)   prostrate (*line 132*)

8 Anita Perez knew 'that it was her duty to get married, when, if she was lucky, this hard life in cocoa would cease' (*lines 18–19*). Do you think people you know expect marriage to save them from boredom and hardship?

Read the newspaper article below. It is part of an interview with Renate Olins of the Marriage Guidance Council.

RELATING TO OTHERS

·MARRIAGE·

Most people don't know if they're happy most of the time, but most people are reasonably content. The most it's reasonable to expect is contentment with occasional flickers of happiness.

There is, she thinks, still a strong difference in attitude between social classes. 'Many working class people have much more separate marriages. The man expects to go out on his own with friends, and the wife expects to go out with her friends. Doing everything together is a mostly middle class idea.'

She notes the changes in attitudes over the last few years. 'Young people of all social classes have higher hopes of an equal partnership in marriage. But most of us tend to revert back to the patterns of our parents, however hard we try to break that mould. Women are a lot more unhappy than they were. They have become more ambitious, but they still don't have the scope to fulfil their ambitions. A lot of dreams are peddled about how much better women's role is, but it isn't. Women's expectations of marriage have risen more than men's. They want their men to be pretty good, and equal. Quite right too, but there's no doubt it makes things more difficult.'

She found it hard to describe what makes marriages work without analysing what makes marriages break down. 'Two things rank highest,' she says, 'disappointment with a partner, or contempt for a partner. People make a mistake when they marry if they think they can change and mould their partner. They are disappointed when they find they can't.'

'People need to be bound together by some level of mutual regard. Admiration isn't necessary – but regard is – a sense that the other is worth listening to and taking into account. Once that has gone, and contempt takes its place, it's very hard to rebuild. If one partner despises the other, you can tell quite soon. They may not say so but you can feel it in their attitude, and it's often painful to see.'

One crucial ingredient, she thinks, is the couple's aspirations. 'They must have the same ambitions, the same expectations from life. It doesn't matter where each has come from, but it matters a great deal that they are both headed in the same direction. Often it turns out that they both assumed quite different things about how they would live.'

In some ways, she thinks, marriage has become a lot harder than it was. Now people only really marry in pursuit of happiness, and their expectations are very high – perhaps too high.

Most people are frightened of loneliness.

The Guardian

RELATING TO OTHERS

9 Renate Olins says that:

Young people of all social classes have higher hopes of an equal partnership in marriage. (*lines 9–10*)

Discuss this suggestion with a friend or in a small group and then

a **either**
Write down some of the qualities you would like your ideal husband or wife to have.

or
Explain why you yourself would not wish to be married.

b Explain what you understand by 'an equal partnership' and why you would or would not want your marriage to be such a partnership.

10 The newspaper extract concludes with the statement:

Most people are frightened of loneliness.

either
Write an essay on the advantages or disadvantages of being alone.

or
Describe the real or imagined life of someone you know who is lonely. The description could take the form of a short story.

11
LOOKING AT OTHER PEOPLE

◆

In Unit 9 (page 88) there is an obituary, by a journalist. The obituary below is written from a poet's point of view. It was inspired by a notice in the local newspaper about the death of someone with the same name as the poet.

Nicholson, Suddenly

From the *Barrow Evening Mail*, Thurs. 13 Feb. 1969

> 'NICHOLSON—(Suddenly) on February 11, Norman, aged 57 years, beloved husband of Mona Nicholson, and dear father of Gerald, of 6 Atkinson Street, Haverigg, Millom.'

So Norman Nicholson is dead!
I saw him just three weeks ago
Standing outside a chemist's shop,
His smile alight, his cheeks aglow,
I'd never seen him looking finer: 5
'I can't complain at all,' he said,
'But for a touch of the old angina.'
Then hobbled in for his prescription.
Born in one town, we'd made our start,
Though not in any way related,   10
Two years and three streets apart,
Under one nominal description:
'Nicholson, Norman,' entered, dated,
In registers of birth and school.
In 1925 we sat   15
At the same desk in the same class —
Me, chatty, natty, nervous, thin,
Quick for the turn of the teacher's chin:
Silent, shy and smiling, he,
And fleshed enough for two of me —   20
An unidentical near twin
Who never pushed his presence in

LOOKING AT OTHER PEOPLE

When he could keep it out.
                    For seven
Years after that each neither knew,
Nor cared much, where or even whether
The other lived. And then, together,
We nearly booked our berths to heaven: —
Like a church weathercock, *I* crew
A graveyard cough and went to bed
For fifteen months: *he* dropped a lead
Pipe on his foot and broke them both.
They wheeled him home to his young wife
Half-crippled for the rest of his life.

In three decades or more since then
We met, perhaps, two years in ten
In shops or waiting for a bus;
Greeted each other without fuss;
Just: 'How do, Norman?' — Didn't matter
Which of us spoke — we said the same.
And now and then we'd stop to natter:
'How's the leg?' or 'How's the chest?' —
He a crock below the waist
And me a crock above it.

                    Blessed
Both with a certain home-bred gumption,
We stumped our way across the cobbles
Of half a lifetime's bumps and roughness —
He short in step and me in wind,
Yet with a kind of wiry toughness.
Each rather sorry for the other,
We chose the road that suited best —
Neither inscribed the sky with flame;
Neither disgraced the other's name.

And now, perhaps, one day a year
The town will seem for half a minute
A place with one less person in it,
When I remember I'll not meet
My unlike double in the street.
Postmen will mix us up no more,
Taking my letters to his door,
For which I ought to raise a cheer.
But can I stir myself to thank

LOOKING AT OTHER PEOPLE

My lucky stars, when there's a blank
Where his stars were? For I'm left here,   65
Wearing his name as well as mine,
Finding the new one doesn't fit,
And though I'll make the best of it,
Sad that such things had to be —
But glad, still, that it wasn't me.   70

Norman Nicholson

Suggested activities

1 Discuss with a partner or in a small group what you liked or disliked about the poem. Note down any lines or phrases that you particularly liked or disliked.

2 The poem provides a lot of information about the two Norman Nicholsons. Discuss what you learn about both of them with a partner, and together decide:

a in what ways they were similar,
b in what ways they were different.

3 Although the poem is inspired by the memory of the dead man, the poet tells us some things about himself. Using the information which you found in answer to question 2, and anything else that seems relevant, write a paragraph about the poet from the *other man's* point of view.

4 Invent an alternative title for the poem and say why you think your title is a good one.

5 Re-write the poem as a brief obituary. You should use the facts mentioned in the poem and you may, if you wish, assume the same point of view as the poet, Norman Nicholson.

6 The poet describes the other Norman as

'An unidentical near twin' (*line 21*)

and later comments that

           'I'll not meet
My unlike double in the street.
Postmen will mix us up no more
Taking my letters to his door.'   (*lines 58–61*)

Are you ever mistaken for anybody else? Have you got, or would you like to have, an 'unlike double'? There must be occasions when it would be very useful to blame somebody else with the same name! Write a story or a play about such an incident. Here are some ideas which may help you.

LOOKING AT OTHER PEOPLE

a   There might be someone with the same name as you who attends the same school, but who is *either* always in trouble *or* extremely well behaved. Yet again, you are mistaken for each other, and your story or play should be based on the results.

b   You have been summoned to an interview or to an important meeting, but there is a mistake and your namesake goes instead. What happens?

c   One of the two doubles suddenly becomes well known, as, for example, a film star, footballer, singer, writer, mountaineer, politician or criminal. Does the other try to cash in on the fame or attempt to live it all down?

You may have other ideas. However you choose to present your story, remember to describe the differences and similarities in both appearance and character of the two people so that the reader can really imagine what they were like. Only the names of the two people need to be identical – their attitudes and behaviour may be as different as you like to make them.

7   Study the picture opposite very carefully. The photographer used no words but managed to convey a great deal of information about this woman and her character through the picture.

a   What emotions do you think the woman is experiencing?
b   Does she appear downcast or cheerful?
c   Is she prosperous or poverty-stricken?
d   What impression do you receive about the woman from the way in which she is seated, her clothing, her surroundings?
e   When you have thought carefully about the picture, write the opening paragraph of a story about the woman and choose a title.

8   In question 7, you examined a picture for clues to a woman's personality.

a   Assemble your own collection of pictures from newspapers, magazines and books which also reveal details of character. Try to include pictures of people showing a range of emotions – fear, excitement, rage, guilt, joy, happiness, and so on.

b   Look at what the people are doing, what they are wearing, how they are standing or sitting or moving.
   What connections do they seem to have with others in the same picture?
      What conversation or arguments might they be having?
      What has just happened to them? What could happen next?

c   When you have collected about six pictures (if necessary include a photograph of yourself), exchange pictures among a

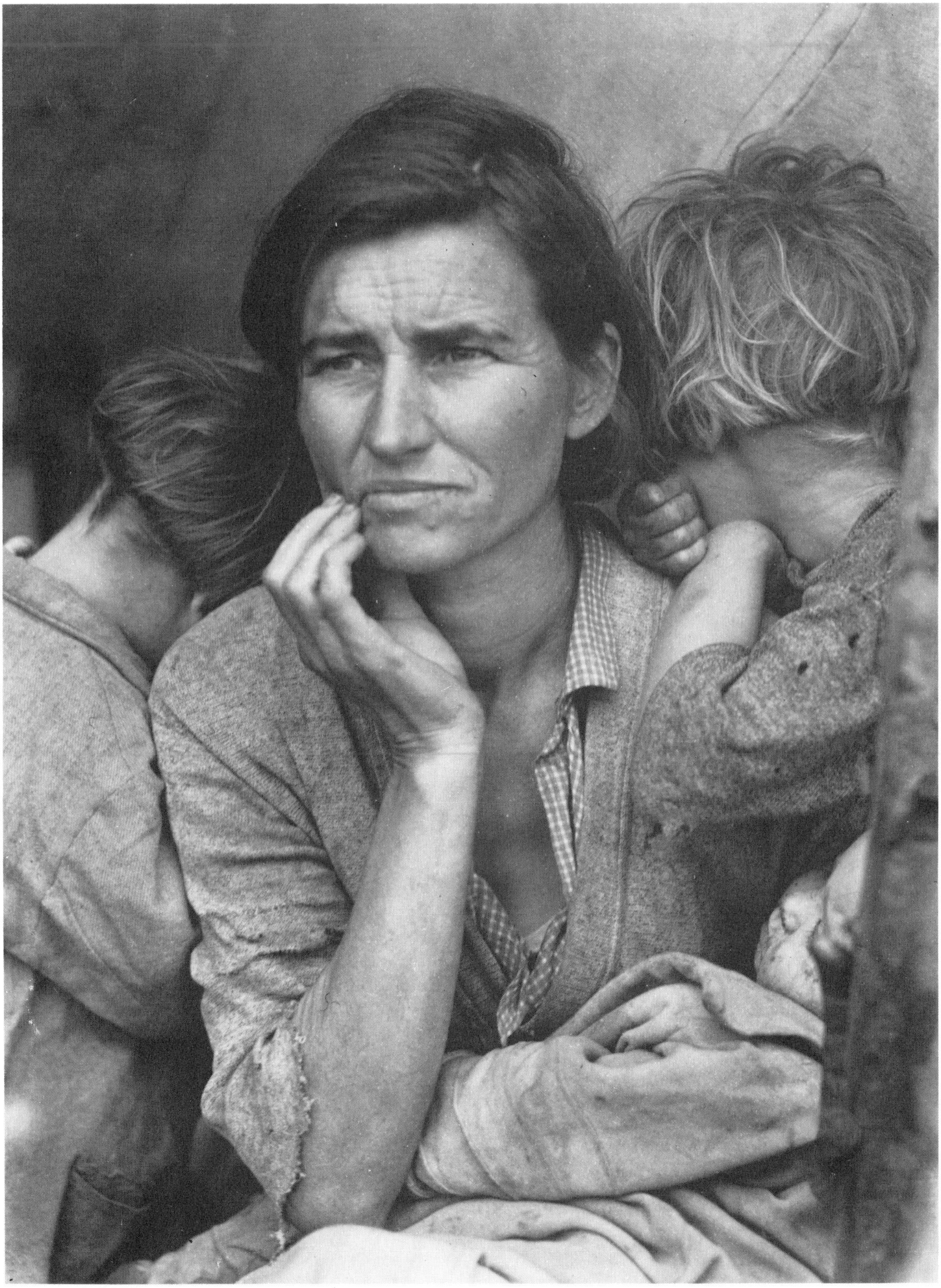

LOOKING AT OTHER PEOPLE

group of two or three of your friends.
   Each person should select any two pictures from another's collection and describe, *aloud*, the scenes in as much detail as possible. Do not write anything down, but keep up a running commentary for at least three minutes. You may say anything you like about the pictures so long as there is some clear connection between your ideas and the actual scene.

d Exchange your selected pictures for those of a friend, and then study one of them for about a minute. Without looking at the picture again, try to remember as many details as you can.

e Compose a caption for all the pictures.

Read the two poems printed below. In the first poem, Elizabeth Jennings is writing about people who are now dead and who were never well known. In the second poem, J.C. Hall is writing about people whom he once loved and who are now elsewhere.

In Memory of Anyone Unknown to Me

At this particular time I have no one
Particular person to grieve for, though there must
Be many, many unknown ones going to dust
Slowly, not remembered for what they have done
Or left undone. For these, then, I will grieve   5
Being impartial, unable to deceive.

How they lived or died is quite unknown,
And, by that fact gives my grief purity –
An important person quite apart from me
Or one obscure who drifted down alone.   10
Both or all I remember, have a place.
For these I never encountered face to face.

Sentiment will creep in. I cast it out
Wishing to give these classical repose,
No epitaph, no poppy and no rose   15
From me, and certainly no wish to learn about
The way they lived or died. In earth or fire
They are gone. Simply because they were human, I admire.

Elizabeth Jennings

LOOKING AT OTHER PEOPLE

Persons Once Loved

Persons once loved are loved in a sense always.
They go yet never depart. Their times are driven
So deep we keep the occasions, like birthdays
That come round year after year though nothing's given.

Four or five women have cut their names in my heart.   5
Remembering one's not disloyal to the others.
The paradox is, however much they've hurt,
Or we've hurt them, they're still in a way our lovers.

Impossible not to wonder how they are
Or who they're with or whether our fashions linger   10
In what they do — like the ache of a limb not there
Or a wedding ring stuck fast on a widowed finger.

J.C. Hall

9 When you have read the two poems carefully, discuss the attitudes of the two poets towards their subjects. Set out your conclusions in two separate paragraphs, using reference and quotation to support whatever conclusions you reach. Think in particular about why the poets are remembering the people in the poems.

10 Describe an individual who has made a very deep impression on you. It may be someone for whom you have an intense dislike or great admiration, or even someone you have never met but whose achievements have impressed you.

12
COPING WITH THE WORLD

Judy Urquhart, the author of the following passages, chose to live in a remote country area with her husband. They practised 'self-sufficiency', which meant that they provided all that they needed for themselves. They found their own shelter, and they had to hunt for or pick all their own food. She later wrote a magazine article about their experiences and a book entitled 'Living off Nature', full of practical information for other people. (The passages have been arranged in sections with questions and discussion topics separating them.)

LIVING OFF NATURE

We settled near Dulverton, where we had been offered the run of a grassy valley which was soon to be flooded to make a reservoir. It had a small trout stream running through the middle, oak and beech woods on either side, Exmoor above and a wooden hut some Boy Scouts had built a few years before. Perfect, we thought, and certainly better than the alternative of a moor in Scotland covered with nothing but heather. Nonetheless it was not ideal.

We planned to live off the land for two months only and we chose to go in August and September when, though many green leaves would be past their prime, berries, fungi and wild animals would be there in plenty. We also had the basics of a goat, four hens, a bag of crushed oats, a knife, an axe, snares, matches, a cooking pot, a change of clothing, a sleeping bag and books. I brought honey from my bees and candles, soap, salt and wine which I had made at home. We planned to make other things, like clothes, baskets, plates, pottery, paper and so on, while we were there.

The first night was bleak. The goat escaped; bracken on an ill swept floor was very different from a bed; and it rained. The rain continued almost unabated for ten days, rations were scarce and uncooked owing to a lack of fire and I came to the conclusion that if this was what surviving meant I would rather not.

COPING WITH THE WORLD

Suggested activity

1 The author gives a list of the basic items which they took with them. Do you think they were the right things to take? Would you have taken anything different?

THE DAILY ROUND

When the weather cleared and stayed clear, the goat had been caught and become a friend and we had established a good routine, I came gradually to find pleasure in the daily routine of getting up, milking the goat, feeding the hens, eating a breakfast of oatcakes, honey and milk, fetching drinking water from the spring, getting wood and foraging for food. At first we would go for a long walk hoping to identify edible plants on the way, but as we became more familiar with the country we would make for certain known spots: places in the woods where there were good fungi, a part of the stream where watercress grew profusely, the edge of the moor thick with brambles, a clearing in the wood full of wild raspberries, a lane with an abundance of dandelion leaves and a meadow with more sorrel, yarrow and valerian than grass. After lunch we either lazed away in the sun with a book or spent the time weaving baskets, making pottery or other similar tasks. Then in early evening Brendan would disappear to lay snares or to shoot a squirrel, rabbit or pigeon. This I would be given to cook, after the skin or feathers had been removed and put aside for treatment. Fishing was also an evening occupation; sometimes we would take a further walk for food. The goat was milked again and then we would light a fire, cook oatcakes and whatever else was for dinner, drink some wine and, as September advanced and the nights drew in, light a candle. But bedtime was always early and the candle was not alight for long.

In fact we slept a great deal. Partly because of all the fresh air and exercise but also because of a lack of food. Even when there was enough, the monotony of the diet drove away appetite. In spite of this we remained very healthy but both of us lost weight and the deficiency affected us in other ways too. I remember taking many rests during walks up hills, we had little energy and were uninventive. We failed to do many of the things we had intended to do, or could have done, if our minds had been full of their usual supply of ideas. The daily routine eventually became boring because it was always the same, devoted to the same pursuits – finding food and keeping dry and warm. I think perhaps this kind of life works best with a group of people. The work load could be spread and there would be a variety of company; it is extraordinarily difficult for anyone used to a modern urban

COPING WITH THE WORLD

environment with all its diverse entertainment to adapt suddenly to a completely different way of life — if you are used to outside stimulation you have withdrawal symptoms when it is removed.

As compensation there was the utter peace and beauty of the valley and the surrounding country. The feeling that if you wanted to sit and stare all day there was nothing — no telephone, no appointments, no radio with the news, no need to look smart — to prevent you doing it. We were able to think and read with a concentration and pleasure never before experienced. And as a couple we got on rather better than usual, the reason being, I think, that we relied totally on each other for survival.

40

Further activities

2
a   What do you think are the advantages and the disadvantages of this way of life? Discuss whether you would like to try it or whether you think it is madness in the closing years of the twentieth century.

b   Look carefully at the second paragraph where the author suggests that 'this kind of life works best with a group of people'. Consider the reasons she gives for this. Do you agree?

3 Work with a group and imagine that you are all to live together as self-sufficiently as possible away from towns and villages. Consider these questions:

a   When and where would you go?
b   What sort of area would you choose?
c   What would you take?
d   How long would you go for?
e   How many people would you go with?

If you can think of any actual places, consider carefully if they would be suitable or not. You will find it helpful to read the section below, 'Choosing a site'.

When you have decided on your site, real or imaginary, discuss in your group what work would have to be done and how you would share the work out among the members of the group. How would you make sure that everybody worked as hard as everybody else? How would disagreements be settled? Would you need to draw up any rules?

When you have decided these matters, and any others that seem important to you, compose a diary (written or taped) recording what happens, what you achieved and how you get on with each other.

CHOOSING A SITE

Were I to start again, I would choose a site by a river and within easy reach of the sea. A southern site would be better than a northern one; the summer is longer, the winter less cold and the vegetation and wild life more varied and lush. The Isle of Purbeck in Dorset, the south of Wales where Carmarthen and Pembroke meet, the country round the Solway Firth, the part nearest the coast of the Lammermuir Hills in Scotland or parts of the south-west of England and the south of Ireland are all places where, within a ten-mile radius, there are enough of the right geographical features to make total survival in the wild possible. They all have streams and rivers which run into estuaries, a coast-line with sand and rocks, woods, arable land and upland. In such situations it should be possible to find everything necessary for living wild in a northerly climate.

From the springs and rivers you would get drinking water and freshwater fish: trout, perch, bream and carp. There would also be water-loving plants like watercress for salads and soup and willow trees for basket work.

To be near a large wood of deciduous trees is essential as wood is the basic raw material from which to build your house, make furniture, implements and utensils and, most important, to provide cooking fuel and heat. Most fungi grow in woods; deer, pigeon, pheasant and squirrels live there, and often swarms of wild bees too, in hollow trees.

Access to arable land would be useful, especially if you decided to continue with the way of life, as you would want to start some form of agriculture and keep some animals. The logic of agriculture is obvious: you can dictate what you eat rather than having to take a chance on what nature offers. Arable land is the natural home of many wild plants and of those cultivated ones which have escaped, often not very far, especially cereals and oil plants. Partridge, pigeons and small birds feed on arable land. In most parts of the country fields are surrounded by hedges. In these you will usually find the best brambles, sloes, crab apples, elderberries and haws. A hedgerow is the best place for laying traps, as rabbits and other small animals live in them. Ditches in between fields often have the best nettles for eating and cloth-making.

Upland is usually rough land; there you find bracken – edible and good for bedding and potash too – useful trees like rowan and birch and plants such as heather and bilberry. In the grassy bits you will find thyme, eyebright and speedwell for flavouring beer and, most certainly, rabbit warrens. In the wooded areas on the hillside badgers dig their sets; on the moorland live curlew, grouse and larks.

COPING WITH THE WORLD

An estuary is the ideal place to evaporate salt and is the home of many molluscs, fish and water birds. A coast consisting of a mixture of rock and sand will have more seaweed and molluscs and as many fish as any other combination. If there are cliffs there will be gulls nesting in them; they and their eggs are well worth eating; the small feathers can be used for stuffing and the larger ones, if you have no geese, for quills. Clay is most easily dug from cliffs where a cross-section of geological deposits is exposed. From clay you can make pots and containers for cooking and storage. Ideally you would have a source of limestone too; this is the best building stone and also provides lime, used in so many articles. If there was metal as well your site would be complete.

The exact position of the house would be decided by the water supply. It would be near a spring for drinking water; preferably, one which develops into a stream so that once you became established a supply could be piped into the house. I would begin by building only a rudimentary shelter — a gipsy tent or a dugout and I would live in this to see how life was developing before building myself a more substantial structure. But both would be in places not too exposed to the west wind and on well-drained ground.

After establishing water and shelter the next consideration would be wood for fuel. The source of this should be close by as surprisingly large quantities are needed for even small amounts of cooking and heating. When we lived off the land we only had a fire in the evenings and even so we spent one or two days a week gathering fuel.

You will, for preference, begin your survival time in late spring or summer when wild food is at its most abundant and day-to-day eating is no problem. Your only worry should be to manage to preserve enough of the surplus to keep you through the lean winter months. Winter is the time when you will be most free to spin wool, weave, make baskets and carve wood into implements and utensils — a store of basic materials out of which these can be made should be put aside during the summer.

Further activities

4 Few of us, if any, live off nature as the author of this passage set out to do. Few of us, nowadays, belong to a family which actually produces all its own food or makes all its own clothes and household equipment. We buy what we need from shops and we pay with money which we have earned in some way.

a How do you think *you* would manage if you could not buy what you needed from a nearby shop or supermarket?

b Think carefully about the many things that you use every day and make a list of the essential items under headings like food, drink, clothing, and compare your list with those compiled by others in the class.

COPING WITH THE WORLD

5 Are there any things on your list that you could make yourself, or for which you could find a substitute?

   a Bread is considered an essential food, and millions of loaves are bought every day. Read the instructions for bread-making given below and, if possible, have a go at baking it yourself.

Ingredients (for one large and one small loaf)
25 g (1 oz) fresh yeast *or*
15 g (½ oz) dried yeast *and*
1 teaspoon sugar
500 ml (¾ pint) warm water
750 g (1½ lb) strong flour
1 rounded teaspoon salt
15 g (½ oz) lard

Method
1. Gradually blend water into fresh yeast *or* Dissolve sugar in water; stir in dried yeast; leave in warm place for 10–15 minutes until frothy.
2. Mix together flour and salt in a large bowl.
3. Rub in fat.
4. Use a palette knife to stir in yeast liquid. If necessary add more flour or more liquid to make a firm dough.
5. Turn dough onto lightly floured surface, and knead by folding dough towards you, then pushing away with palm of hand until firm and elastic – about 10 minutes. Shape into a ball.
6. Place dough in bowl, cover with lightly oiled polythene and leave in a warm place to rise until double in size – 1–1½ hours.
7. Turn risen dough onto lightly floured surface, and knead until firm – about 2 minutes.
8. Divide dough into 2 or 3 pieces, and shape to half-fill lightly greased tins. Cover with lightly oiled polythene and leave in a warm place until the dough is just rounded over the top of the tins – about 45 minutes.
9. Uncover and brush top of loaves with beaten egg and water or milk.
10. Bake in a pre-heated oven 230°C, 450°F, Gas mark 8, for 30–40 minutes, until golden brown. When bread is cooked, it should sound hollow if tapped on base.
11. Remove bread from tins, and cool on wire rack.

If you buy a pack of prepared dough or bread mix, follow the instructions on the packet.

   b After you have tried baking bread, write a short report on your progress, saying whether you enjoyed making it and what the end product actually tasted like. Would you be better off going to the baker's for your bread in future?

COPING WITH THE WORLD

6 There are many products and skills for which we rely on other people. You will have mentioned some of them in your answer to question 4. It *is* possible for non-specialists to produce these goods or acquire these skills. The list below suggests a few of the activities which can be useful in and around the home. You may be able to think of others.

Growing your own vegetables   Woodwork and carpentry
Keeping chickens   Painting and decorating
Knitting   Repairing the car
Dressmaking   Making your own radio
Wine and beer making

7 Prepare a short talk for the class on some skill or pastime that you have; and, if possible, show your class how it is done.
    Write down brief and clear instructions. You might do this stage by stage as in the recipe for making bread. When you do this, it is worth noting the special style of the language used in the recipe. What is unusual about it?

8 It is impossible to say whether the people who 'lived off nature' got more satisfaction out of what they did than many of us do today. Read the following poem which is about a man who does a particular job without finding much satisfaction in what he does.

The Holiday, and After

He left suit and stiff collar behind,
   put on red jeans, hat, tattered vest,
and dug praties in wildest Ireland.

   Blue winds sliced through the hills,
the peat bog sucked and settled lower   5
   in its ancient bed

and in two weeks he grew a new face,
   took on the skin of a creature
making out in the wilderness

   Back at the Bank he flicked notes   10
with a pimpled rubber thumb
   and ticked off the days

on a company calendar
   as the ice battalions of Winter
advanced across the town.   15

COPING WITH THE WORLD

   And then, while stacking others' cash,
he felt the walls of commerce split
   and through the cracks

watched new beasts come.
   In the cage of his chest   20
his heart thumped like a bunched fist

   as he saw them come on slow
through rough streets littered with whitening
      bones
   and the first of a new year's snow.

                              Wes Magee

a What do you think that the poet is trying to suggest by contrasting how the man dresses when at work and how he dressed on holiday?

b Explain what you think that the poet means or suggests by the following:

   1 . . . in two weeks he grew a new face,
         took on the skin of a creature
      making out in the wilderness (*lines 7–9*)

   2   Back at the Bank he flicked notes
      with a pimpled rubber thumb
         and ticked off the days (*lines 10–12*)

   3   In the cage of his chest
      his heart thumped like a bunched fist
         (*lines 20–21*)

   4   as he saw them come on slow
      through rough streets littered with whitening
         bones (*lines 22–3*)

9

a At the beginning of the story called 'The Pigeon Cree' (page 62) we learn something of Geordie's attitude to his job. How would you compare it to the attitude of the man in the above poem?

b How do the job and the attitude of the man in Wes Magee's poem differ from those of the men in this next poem?

Cathedral Builders

They climbed on sketchy ladders towards God,
With winch and pulley hoisted hewn rock into heaven,
Inhabited sky with hammers, defied gravity,
Deified stone, took up God's house to meet Him.

And came down to their suppers and small beer; 5
Every night slept, lay with their smelly wives,
Quarrelled and cuffed the children, lied,
Spat, sang, were happy or unhappy,

And every day took to the ladders again;
Impeded the rights of way of another summer's 10
Swallows, grew greyer, shakier, became less inclined
To fix a neighbour's roof of a fine evening

Saw naves sprout arches, clerestories soar,
Cursed the loud fancy glaziers for their luck,
Somehow escaped the plague, got rheumatism, 15
Decided it was time to give it up.

To leave the spire to others; stood in the crowd
Well back from the vestments at the consecration,
Envied the fat bishop his warm boots,
Cocked up a squint eye and said, 'I bloody did that'. 20

John Ormond

COPING WITH THE WORLD

Further activities

10

a What do you think the poet means by the following?

(They)   Inhabited sky with hammers, defied gravity,
Deified stone, took up God's house to meet him, (*lines 3–4*)

Impeded the rights of way of another summer's
Swallows . . . (*lines 10–11*)

b Although these men were the builders of God's House, they themselves were very ordinary men. Explain how the poet suggests their ordinariness.

c Pick out two lines or parts of lines which tell us that the building of the cathedral took a long time. Explain why you chose those particular lines.

d Make up an imaginary conversation between two of the builders *either* while they are at work *or* at the consecration ceremony. (If you need guidance on setting out conversation, turn to page 44.)

11 Imagine that one of the builders referred to in this poem deposits his wages at the bank mentioned in 'The Holiday and After'. (Do not worry that the poems refer to different periods of history.) What would the cathedral builder and the bank clerk think of each other? Write a description of one of these men from the other man's point of view, or use their meeting as the basis for a play or a story. Provide your own title.

13
LOVING ONE ANOTHER

♦

This story is an account by a woman of something that happened when she was fifteen. She describes life in Canada with her mother and her relationship with her boyfriend. She recalls a particular incident when she learned 'one of the truths about love'.

At the time of this story I was living in Canada. It was towards the end of the Second World War, and I was nearly sixteen — a rather uncomfortable mixture of child and woman, Canadian and English. My mother and I had been evacuated five years before to Saskatoon, Saskatchewan — euphemistically known as the Hub City of the Prairies — and had only during the last two grown accustomed to the flat sameness of the wheatfields, the vast space between towns broken by the stark, jutting grain elevators, white in the dry clear air.

We had even grown fond of Saskatoon itself; but it was always with relief that we escaped, during the baking hot months of the summer holidays, to one of the scattered lakes north of Prince Albert. Pushed like thumb-prints into the all-but-unexplored Northern forests, the sheltered rims of these lakes accommodated occasional groups of log cabins in which farmers, woodsmen and summer visitors shared the peace and beauty of the woods with the teeming wild life that belonged there.

In these magic surroundings we used to spend long summer days in the open air, swimming and canoeing, walking, reading, or just lying dreaming in the sun. In the evenings the three-foot pine logs would burn with their blue flames and sweet smell, and we would sit and talk, listening to the piano students playing in the next cabin and the bitterns creaking in the reeds, or watch the fireflies, millions of them, dancing in the fringe of trees between our porch and the Lake, which was always a bright, luminous grey after the unbelievable sunset colours had faded.

LOVING ONE ANOTHER

That last summer before we returned to England was particularly enchanted. For one thing, I was in love for the first time. No one will ever convince me that one cannot be in love at fifteen. I loved then as never since, with all my heart and without doubts or reservations or artifice. Or at least, that is how I loved by the end of the summer. When we left for the Lake in June, it was all just beginning.

My boyfriend worked in Saskatoon, but the Lake was 'his place' — the strange and beautiful wilderness drew him with an obsessive urgency, so I cannot claim it was only to see me that he got on his motor-cycle as many Fridays as he possibly could, and drove three hundred-odd miles along the pitted prairie roads to spend the weekend with us.

Sometimes he couldn't come, and then the joy would go out of everything until Monday, when I could start looking forward to Friday again. He could never let us know in advance, as we were too far from civilization to have a phone or even a telegraph service, so that it wasn't until noon on Saturdays that I had to give up hope. Three hundred miles in those conditions is quite a journey. Besides, Don was hard up, and sometimes worked overtime at weekends.

But except for those lost and empty Saturdays and Sundays, I was deliriously happy. So happy that I began to think, for the first time in years, quite a lot about God. After Don had managed to come for several consecutive weekends, I came to the conceited conclusion that God was taking personal care of me. I talked to Him as if to a companion, and somewhere in that maze of hot, contemplative days, when God, or nature, or whatever you care to call the abstract Power of the world, seemed almost tangibly close, I conceived the idea that if I posed a direct question the first answer that came into my mind would be the correct one.

The childishness of this faith-game is easy to deride now; the fact remains that it worked. I used to try it out on simple things; 'Will it rain tomorrow?' 'Will there be a letter from England today?' – and, most often of all, 'Will Don come this week?' At first I used to be a little confused by the jumble of negative and affirmative thoughts that would rush through my mind, but after a while there would be a little space of whirling blankness, and then a yes or a no would flash forth quite clearly, and if it ever proved wrong, I don't remember it. Except for the last time.

One Monday morning I was sitting at the end of our little canoe-jetty with one foot trailing in the warm water, watching the tiny fish prodding at it inquisitively with their transparent noses, when my mother came down to me, stepping over the gaping holes in the planking.

'Did you borrow a five-dollar bill out of my cash-box?' she asked.

'No . . .' I replied, stirring idly with my foot and watching the little fish flicker away.

'Funny,' she said. 'I must have put it somewhere else.'

She went away, and I lay back on the planking, feeling it warm and rough through my shirt, and behind my sun-baked eyelids relived the past two days, moment by moment. After a while, my mother came back. Her hollow footsteps behind me had a worried urgency that made me sit up.

'I can't find it,' she said. There was a little knot of muscles between her eyebrows.

'I'll come and help you look.'

'It's no good,' she said, pushing me back. 'I remember now, I *did* put it in the box. There's nowhere else it could be.'

'Well, what's happened to it?'

'I don't know,' she said. She stood beside me, frowning across the bright, flat water.

I should explain that Don was not the only person who used to visit us. We had many friends, and weekends at the Lake during the heat of July were considered well worth the long train journey and the uncomfortable truck ride involved in reaching us. Lots of local people used to pop in too, as well as neighbours from near-by cabins. During the weekend just past, there had been a good half-dozen people on the premises besides Don.

I find it quite impossible to this day to understand why the thought that Don might have taken the five dollars should even have crossed my mind. But it did, and at once a cold pall of self-loathing fell on me. I shivered in the glittering heat, and my mother bent and put her arm round me.

LOVING ONE ANOTHER

'Don't worry, darling,' she said. 'We can't be sure anyone took it.'

'But they're all friends,' I mumbled. What had occurred to me would never in a hundred years have occurred to her; she would as soon have suspected *me* of stealing as Don. She said: 'Anyone could have come in and taken it while we were over at the reef.' But there were no strangers, and she knew it. The lakeside population is a tiny, isolated community, which no tramps or wanderers ever invade.

Five dollars was a respectable sum to us in those days, with only our meagre allowance from England to live on. But my mother was never one to cry over spilt milk, and she told me to forget all about it.

But I couldn't. I think it was guilt at that flash of involuntary disloyalty that kept the thing alive in my mind. I hated myself for giving it a first thought, let alone a second, and as the days went by the silly, groundless suspicion grew, and my guilt with it, the one feeding the other. The happiness of our surroundings was utterly spoilt, and so was the former delight of forward-looking; I felt I couldn't look Don in the face again, and almost dreaded the coming weekend. And yet I could not shake off this feeling of doubt, which lay on my spirit like a guilty burden.

At first I refused to apply my newly found 'test', because to do so would be to admit the doubt to myself, at a time when I was still desperately trying to pretend it was not there at all; and then, when I reached the stage of having to admit it, I was afraid to 'ask' because I knew I would believe the answer.

But by Friday I was so wretched in my self-created hell that I could bear it no longer. I went away by myself on to the shore; the evening air was unusually heavy, and the placid water had an almost ominous beauty. I stood looking at the dying sunset, beyond the trees' ragged silhouette. It was beautiful – too beautiful for me, at that moment. I didn't feel fit to look at it. I started to cry in great, dry sobs, and suddenly I said aloud:

'Did Don take the five dollars?'

And the answer came quite clearly, 'Yes.'

The storm broke with the uncanny abruptness of all weather changes in that land of extremes. One minute the accentuated reds and lemons of the sunset were smeared across the west; the next, the blackness of thunderclouds had obliterated them, and the leaden bowl of the sky was fissured with lightning which spread in infinite detail, like the veins of a leaf. It vanished, leaving me blinking in the sudden darkness; then came the thunder, and the next second the flat face of the Lake was dancing in angry peaks and the pines were lashing like whips.

I tried not to expect Don that night. I felt that my thoughts might have communicated themselves to him somehow, and that, sensing my treachery, he wouldn't come. But it was ironic that, convinced, irrationally, as I now was, of his guilt, I should nevertheless have longed to see him as I never had before.

LOVING ONE ANOTHER

I lay in bed under the sloping roof of the cabin and listened to the rain beating like multiple hammers over my head, feeling the wind shake the cabin to its foundations with one ferocious impact after another, watching the black square of window light up with blinding suddenness and frequency. Once I got up and stood looking out over the treetops, shivering; when the flashes came, they showed the solid forest swaying with the flexibility of a wheatfield.

I experienced a loneliness of spirit unequalled by anything I have felt since. My strange betrayal hurt in a sharp and basic way which would be impossible now, through the layers of self-protective insulation the years have laid on my heart.

I crawled back into bed, trying to close my throat against the tears. But when my mother, prompted by the sweet deep affinity between us, came in to me, she kissed my cheek and found it wet.

'Don't cry, sweetie,' she said softly. 'He may still come.'

'I don't want him to!' I sobbed before I could stop myself, and when, startled, she drew back and said 'But why?' I had to lie, and say it was because I was afraid for him, riding through the storm over bad roads which the rain would now have reduced to sheets of yellow mud.

When she had tucked me in and gone, the lie became true. I lay thinking about the very real danger of those roads . . . you couldn't walk along them safely after heavy rain; your feet would slip from under you on the crude camber. Would he have enough sense to stop and wait until the storm ended? But the roads in Northern Canada are not like the friendly well-populated English ones, where there is always a town or at least a farmhouse within walking distance. You can travel a hundred miles with nothing but the rough road itself to show that you are not the first human being to go that way.

I imagined Don fighting the storm, unwilling to stop in the middle of some sodden wilderness. The strength of the wind buffeting the cabin made the motor-bike, which had always looked to me so heavy and solid, seem in my frightened thoughts frail enough to be blown on to its side by the first gust that struck it. I thought of Don pinned under it, skidding, his face pressed into the yellow clay; I saw the rain beating on the stillness of his young neck above his leather jacket; I heard the coughing of the disabled machine above the fury of the storm.

It was hours later, when I had relived the scene a hundred times, that I suddenly realized the sound of the roaring engine was real. The storm was dying; the wind was no more than a sullen, spasmodic growl through the trees and a steady patter of rain on the roof. I lay absolutely still, relief and panic fighting for ascendancy within me, each in itself overwhelming enough to freeze the breath in my lungs as I heard Don's heavy, tired footsteps on the wooden stairs.

LOVING ONE ANOTHER

He stood in the open doorway. The faint early-dawn light from the window gleamed on his wet black hair, his wet face and the streaming, shiny jacket. He stood for a long moment, his breath labouring, not knowing whether I was awake or asleep. His arms hung wearily at his sides; I could make out his stooped shoulders and hear the faint tapping as water ran off him on to the plank floor.

Then I whispered to him, and stretched out my hand. He came and bent over me, pressing his cold wet face against my hot one. The rain from his hair dripped from my pillow. He tried to keep my hands under the bedclothes, saying 'No, you'll get so wet –' laughing under his breath, holding my hands down with one hand and trying to struggle out of his soaking jacket. But I got free and threw my arms round his neck, pulling him down to me, and he gave in. I felt the wet stiffness of the jacket through my thin pyjamas; his hands, freezing cold, held me close; his icy wet ear was against my cheek, his lips pressed to my shoulder . . . The guilt and the doubt broke up all at once within me, the way the solid surface of the frozen Saskatchewan River breaks up in the spring. The released water rushes along, carrying its broken bonds of ice along in a crashing torrent. That was the sort of *exulting* freedom I felt now I knew the absolute stupidity of my fears.

Most truths are learned gradually, through many small lessons. But the truth about love – or one of the truths, for there are many, and none is absolute except for the person for whom it is real – came rushing in on me in that wet, close, relieving moment. It was this: that it isn't until you have truly doubted someone that you can truly and finally believe in them.

'Don –' I whispered, into his cold ear, all my recent fear in my voice.

'Fathead,' he whispered back tenderly. 'You know I can drive Matilda through an earthquake . . . Go to sleep.' He dried my face with a distant corner of the sheet, turned my pillow over to the dry side, and tucked the bedclothes snugly round me. My hands kept creeping out to touch him, and he kept firmly pushing them back into the warmth. 'Close your eyes,' he ordered. When I did, the long exhaustion swept over me blackly. I fell asleep half-way through a kiss.

The next morning the sun shone brilliantly from a cloudless sky. The Lake was a sheet of luminous glass, and every pine-needle glistened in its cleanness like a shred of green silk. From the earth rose an overwhelming smell of bruised freshness.

The three of us sat on the wired-in porch and drank our morning coffee, watched our almost-tame chipmunks rejoicing on the steaming woodpile, and laughed at the awfulness of the night behind us. My mother, too, it seemed, had lain awake letting her imagination run riot until she heard Don arrive. And the drive, for all Don's pretended nonchalance, had been no pleasure-trip.

'Was it raining when you left Saskatoon?' I asked, and when he said it had been, heaven's hardest, I burst out 'Oh, then why did you come? You needn't have. It was too dangerous . . .'

He pooh-poohed this, and repeated that Matilda could weather the raging Atlantic if she had to. 'Besides,' he added after a moment, 'I *had* to come this weekend.'

Before I could ask why, my mother asked us if we'd walk up to the store for the groceries. It was a rhetorical question; we were holding hands and looking at each other, and she could see it didn't matter to us what we did, so long as we were together. She went into the living-room to collect money and her shopping list. While she was gone, I noticed that Don's eyes had black rings under them; the expression on his face was sober and grown-up. He started to tell me something and then kissed me instead, leaning across the coffee-cups. The sun was blissfully warm on my closed eyelids and on our clasped hands.

My mother called me. Her voice had a funny note in it.

I went in to her. My eyes, unused to the darkness inside the cabin, could not see how she looked; but she was holding the moneybox.

'Look,' she said, holding it out to me.

Inside, lying on top of some one-dollar bills and small change, was another bill for five dollars.

'It's back!' I exclaimed. 'How funny! When do you suppose that could have happened?'

'It wasn't there last night,' she said. She sounded as if her throat were dry.

I laughed at her. 'What nonsense!' I said. 'It must have been. Nobody's been in the house since last night, except us and Don. I'll bet it's been there the whole time.' She didn't answer, and I went on: 'Well, come on, let's have the list and we'll be off before it gets too hot.'

She handed me the list in silence, and then picked out the five-dollar bill. She held it a moment, as if in doubt about giving it to me; impatient to get back to Don I almost grabbed it from her hand, kissed her, and ran back on to the sun-flooded porch.

Don had his back to me. He was hunched up a little, staring with concentration into his empty coffee-cup. As I stood looking down at him, feeling the sun's warmth glowing on my skin like a blessing, I thought: to love someone is lovely, but incomplete. It's trust that rounds love out, making it perfect. I thought of my child's asking game, and shrugged tolerantly at myself as I had been yesterday. I had the answers to all the questions now.

I dropped a kiss on the smooth black head. 'Come on,' I said. 'I've got five dollars. Let's go buy the world.'

Lynne Reid Banks

LOVING ONE ANOTHER

Suggested activities

1 Why do you think that the author calls the story 'Trust'? Is it a good title?

2 Don frequently visited the cabin, but he says, in lines 222–3:

'I *had* to come this weekend.'

Discuss why coming that weekend should be so important for him. What do you think would have happened if he had not come? Make up an alternative ending to the story and choose another title which is appropriate to your alteration.

3 From your reading of the story, what impression do you get of

    a the girl   *b* the girl's mother   *c* Don.

Consider your impressions carefully and then write a paragraph or two about each character.

4 From lines 1–23 write down as many details as you can find about

a Saskatoon and the surrounding region

b the place where the mother and daughter spent their holidays.

5

a Pick out three details of the description of the landscape and the weather from lines 107–27 and explain how they reflect the mood of the girl at that time.

b Find a sentence later in the story where the description of the landscape and weather reflects an entirely different mood.

6 Say what you think is meant by the following sentences and explain the significance of each in the story.

a ... at once a cold pall of self-loathing fell on me (*line 87*)

b ... I should nevertheless have longed to see him as I never had before (*lines 131–2*)

c The guilt and the doubt broke up all at once within me (*lines 190–1*)

d She sounded as if her throat were dry (*line 241*)

7 The author writes about landscape and weather at different points in the story. Select two sentences or phrases which you think are particularly effective. Explain why you think they are effective.

LOVING ONE ANOTHER

8 Make sure that you know the meanings of the following words and then use each word in a separate sentence of your own. Use each word in the same sense as it is used in the story.

teeming (*line 15*)	invade (*line 95*)
luminous (*line 22*)	meagre (*line 97*)
artifice (*line 27*)	ominous (*line 114*)
civilization (*line 38*)	flexibility (*line 139*)
deliriously (*line 43*)	spasmodic (*line 171*)
contemplative (*line 47*)	ascendancy (*line 173*)
tangibly (*line 49*)	overwhelming (*line 173*)

9 In lines 25–7 the writer insists:
'No one will ever convince me that one cannot be in love at fifteen. I loved then as never since, with all my heart and without doubts or reservations or artifice.'

What do you think about the writer's statement?

10 The writer says that she 'began to think, for the first time in years, quite a lot about God' (*lines 43–4*).

Why do you think she says, a few lines later, that 'The childishness of this faith-game is easy to deride now' (*line 51*)?

11 'I was deliriously happy' (*lines 42–3*). Write about a time in your own life when you might have said this.

Suggested group work

12
a A teenager suspects that the person he/she loves is dishonest. He/she writes to a magazine advice column for guidance. Working in pairs, one should write the letter and the other should write the answer.
b Working in groups, write two or three serious letters to such a magazine. Describe situations which really could arise and then prepare answers which genuinely try to be helpful.

It may help you to look at some of the advice columns which appear in some magazines and newspapers.

Arrange your group's letters and answers in a folder for other members of your class to read and discuss.

LOVING ONE ANOTHER

The following poems, 'The Room' and 'Colours', express something of the doubt and anxiety about new love relationships. Read them and decide which you prefer.

The Room

It is the afternoons I remember
those unfixable hours after mid-day
when the eternal winter drags its
grimy rag across the sky
wiping colour from the trees 5
the window was cold and wet
at the finger's touch
outside children played in the snow
you pointed to your brother
and as I squinted through the running 10
pane at the moving figures in the
garden more than once I saw my
own reflection

Quietly we sat bridging the floor
with hands interwoven 15
shyly angled on our knees
and sometimes I would pause a glance
at some corner of the room because
I was afraid of how long the
warmth in your eyes would last 20
we talked of the strange way
in which music picked our thoughts
and wove them into the far memory
of blue shadows across our lives

And Sunday afternoon 25
the glass leaves broke beneath
our feet and we saw the ice-reflected
yoke in the ponds for the cold sun
offered us no more comfort and
the trees spoke no colours in 30
my mind the water slid like
spent silver between the banks
of earth and if I had read all
the great works I still could not
have found the words to offer your 35
eyes the satisfaction they deserved.

LOVING ONE ANOTHER

Colours

When your face
appeared over my crumpled life
at first I understood
only the poverty of what I have.
Then its particular light   5
on woods, on rivers, on the sea,
became my beginning in the coloured world
in which I had not yet had my beginning.
I am so frightened, I am so frightened,
of the unexpected sunrise finishing,   10
of revelations
and tears and the excitement finishing.
I don't fight it, my love is this fear,
I nourish it who can nourish nothing,
Love's slipshod watchman.   15
Fear hems me in.

I am conscious that these minutes are short
and that the colours in my eyes will vanish
when your face sets.

Activities on 'The Room'

13 Explain the situation described in the first verse (*lines 1–13*)

14 How does the poet convey a sense of fear and doubt?

15 In the Canadian story you have read, details of landscape and weather were used to suggest the mood of the characters. Find any lines or groups of lines where the poet has done something similar.

16 Pick out two or three examples of metaphor in the poem and explain the effect of each of your examples. (Turn to page 132 if you are uncertain about metaphor and its uses.)

17 Read the poem aloud. You will probably have noticed that there is only one full stop and that there are no commas. Can you think of any reasons why the poet should have omitted punctuation?

LOVING ONE ANOTHER

18 Decide whether the poem was written by a man or a woman. Then

either
Write briefly on your impressions of the relationship between the poet and the person who is addressed.

or
Write briefly about the relationship from the point of view of the other person.

Activities on 'Colours'

You may find it particularly helpful to discuss this poem with another person or in groups.

19 What do you think the poet suggests by the following?

a my crumpled life (*line 2*)

b ... my beginning in the coloured world
in which I had not yet had my beginning. (*lines 7–8*)

c ... I am so frightened,
of the unexpected sunrise finishing. (*lines 9–10*)

20 Explain what you think is the significance of the title, 'Colours'.

21 This poem is punctuated in a more traditional way. Does this make any difference?

22 Do you think this poem was written by a man or a woman? Does it matter?

General activities

23 Which of the two poems did you like more? Can you say why?

24 Write a story, a play or a poem beginning with one or more lines from either of these poems.

14
THE NEXT GENERATION

'Learning with Father' describes how a young father looks after his baby while his wife goes out to work.

It all seemed so simple. My wife announced she was pregnant from the top of the stepladder. We swapped places and I finished papering the attic ceiling. Before and after are plain for all to see. From then on, it got more complicated. We both had satisfying, well paid jobs. We both had any number of other commitments outside normal working hours. Her job requires evening meetings; she is secretary of this and secretary of that, with minutes to write, letters to answer, people to ring back. I represent a declining inner city Borough on the Greater London Council. On top of County Hall's demands, there are the surgeries for constituents, work for the local Party, invitations to speak, meetings with Young Socialists and tenants' associations. Four nights a week is about average. So who was to stop work and look after this selfish, demanding egotistic savage due in a few months' time? Me, as you will have guessed.

We didn't really take long to decide. We each wrote out a shopping list of the 'plus points' from our jobs and commitments. Hers was longer than mine and that was that. The problem was sticking to it. Both grandmothers muttered 'how sensible', strongly implying that sense and rationality were the last criteria to apply to baby-rearing. Both grandfathers said 'have a drink' strongly implying they needed it more than I did. Our friends reacted with guarded admiration. Feminists toed the party line, 'no other solution for people like you. Make sure you publicise, publicise'. Chauvinists tried to be diplomatic, 'quite right, too. Not for me, though. Don't know how my wife copes. Have another, you'll need it'. Cynics deflated 'so he'll achieve his

THE NEXT GENERATION

suppressed ambition to retire before he's 35'. The midwife brought along a male trainee and was cheerily approving.

In January our son arrived. I started delving deep into my psyche trying to find maternal instincts. I need not have worried. The paraphenalia of the whole baby industry unloaded its cornucopia on the front step. Disposable nappies, double locking safety pins, bottle heaters, sterilising outfit (for his bottles, not us), one piece jumper suits, polystyrene bottle insulators, free samples of food and milk powder. The marketing people in Unilever have got their marbles.

The sheer panic of being on my own with a totally dependent and defenceless fledgling soon subsided. Both grandmothers were still muttering how much easier it was nowadays, no more boiling nappies or rationing. For their benefit I assemble bottle, teat, and retaining collar singlehanded. Next the teat is stuffed into a Jaws-sized mouth. Silence reigns and greed slurps. Grandmothers look suitably impressed.

What's it like being a baby in the last quarter of the twentieth century? He hasn't realised yet that he will be 21 in the year 2000. For him, being two to five months old is one long span of uninterrupted pleasure. All the benefits of technology conspire to separate us from our money and ensure his daily round continues at maximum convenience to himself. The flat is a minefield of 'educational' toys meant to blow his mind with mixtures of shapes, textures and noises. This is great in theory, but I doubt its practice. Simple observation tells me that the only response to a new tangible stimulus comprises grasping it, examining it, thinking about it and slowly but inexorably stuffing as much as possible into his mouth. He then takes a millisecond to discover it's inedible and proceeds to chew away for the hell of it. Boredom comes next, followed by oral rejection so I start again with the next.

And all the time I've got committee papers to read, ceilings to be wallpapered, articles to write, money to earn. Then the Chief Whip wants to know if I can go round a Fire Station next Tuesday. How do you take 7.90 kg of slumbering greed up in a 30 metre hydraulic hoist? Answer, you don't. Meeting the new Housing Manager was simpler. Just dump the lad in the corner of the HM's office, pray he won't be sick all over the new carpet and stuff his towel into his mouth. Like Linus in the Charlie Brown cartoon, the towel is an inseparable solace. Home two hours later, just in time to find a mildly distraught fellow councillor on the step wanting to park her infant so that she can do her bit at the Town Hall unencumbered.

Even a calamity brings new insights. Going out too fast one morning I caught his basket against the door frame. Next thing I saw was a bundle of baby and blanket unravelling itself like a Swiss roll on its way to the floor. The bump on his skull came up the size of an egg before the howling started. By the time we got to casualty he looked shaken but OK, conscious and

THE NEXT GENERATION

very, very angry. In line with my wife's prediction, the doctor didn't take our word for it that only his head had been bumped. Discreetly and without revealing his real intention, ribs, back, stomach, buttocks, legs were all prodded. Since the recognition of the baby battering syndrome, doctors, particularly those in practice for many years, keep a very watchful eye on injuries to babies. Perhaps the explanation is that previously they were told about baby falling over, down the stairs, or off the table. It was reassuring to see this watchful young doctor in action.

At the Health Centre I get guarded looks from mothers and Health Visitors. On my third visit I spotted another forlorn male desperately trying to pacify the smallest but loudest Quadrophonic system on the market. My hopes soared – I Am Not Alone and a close encounter of the paternal kind was odds on. Dejection ensued, as the system's mother came tearing down the corridor, seized it and shut it up with the remedy patented aeons ago by the female of the species. There are some things even a male housewife cannot do.

Simon Turney

Suggested activities

1 When you have read the article, discuss your reactions to it with a partner or in a small group. What do you think the father feels about his baby? Find words or phrases in the passage which suggest what his feelings are.

2
a How did the couple decide which of them would stay with the baby? What factors did they take into account in reaching their decision?
b Do you think they should have taken other factors into account before deciding what to do?

3 From the passage, find the phrases which tell us:
a how he tried to think of himself as filling the role of the mother,
b that he stopped worrying about the baby and settled down,
c what the baby does with new toys.

4 Two sets of grandparents are mentioned in the passage. Make up an imaginary conversation between these grandparents who are discussing the attitudes of the baby's parents. Your conversation could be in two parts, the first part before the birth of the child, when they are wondering how things will work out, and the second part sometime after the birth of the child, when they can see the progress for themselves. Tape-record your conversations if possible.

5 Why do you think the writer found the actions of the doctor in the casualty department 'reassuring' (*lines 68–74*)?

THE NEXT GENERATION

6 Write a summary of the whole passage in about three hundred words. (You will find advice on writing a summary in Unit 9.)

7 Find the following words in the passage, and write down another word which means the same thing. You may use a dictionary if necessary, but make sure that your 'new' word could be used in the 'old' sentence without altering its meaning.

rationality (*line 17*)
criteria (*line 18*)
guarded (*line 20*)
tangible (*line 46*)
inedible (*line 49*)
solace (*line 59*)

distraught (*line 60*)
calamity (*line 62*)
prediction (*line 67*)
forlorn (*line 76*)
pacify (*line 77*)

8 You have read about one father's experience of caring for his baby son. Now read the poem 'Morning Song' in which a mother considers her tiny baby.

Morning Song

Love set you going like a fat gold watch.
The midwife slapped your footsoles, and your bald cry
Took its place among the elements.

Our voices echo, magnifying your arrival. New statue.
In a draughty museum, your nakedness   5
Shadows our safety. We stand round blankly as walls.

I'm no more your mother
Than the cloud that distils a mirror to reflect its own slow
Effacement at the wind's hand.

All night your moth-breath   10
Flickers among the flat pink roses. I wake to listen;
A far sea moves in my ear.

One cry, and I stumble from bed, cow-heavy and floral
In my Victorian nightgown.
Your mouth opens as clean as a cat's. The window square   15

Whitens and swallows its dull stars. And now you try
Your handful of notes;
The clear vowels rise like balloons.

Sylvia Plath

THE NEXT GENERATION

Further activities

9 When you have thought about this poem, which you may want to read several times, look again at the first line.

'Love set you going like a fat gold watch.'

A gold watch is valuable and to be treasured – like a baby. They are items which might mark very special occasions and are rarely given.

Births are special events in families, a gift in themselves. The baby will grow up and time will pass – a watch marks time. A watch needs to be wound in order for it to work; a baby is 'set going' by an act of love between parents, and needs to be tended, or kept 'ticking over' lovingly.

A gold watch often hangs on a chain attached to the owner's waistcoat to avoid loss; tiny babies cling to their parents for comfort and security, and have to be carried carefully. A cheerful baby might look fat and healthy like shining gold.

Sylvia Plath has packed all these suggestions into only nine words. Does the same line suggest other ideas to you?

10 Working in small groups, discuss your impression of the poem. Each one of you should choose two or three lines which you specially like and examine them in detail. What pictures and emotions are conveyed?

Metaphors
similes
personification

These are the commonest forms of *figurative language*, and we usually use these forms to emphasise or to make more vivid what we are saying or writing.

Similes involve a comparision and always contain the words *like* or *as*.

Metaphors describe the idea or activity as if it was actually something else.

The baby wriggled across the floor like a worm. (**simile**)
The baby wormed across the floor. (**metaphor**)

Personification is where we speak or write of something that is not living as if it were a person.

The wind moaned in the trees.
Her exam results hit her so hard she hasn't recovered.

We all use language like this, often without realising it, as when we say that the meat we are eating is as tough as old boots, or that a child is as good as gold. Some metaphors and similes have been used so often that we scarcely notice them when they are used; but when they are used effectively they usually suggest a picture of something to us and make what is said or written more vivid and more memorable. Poetry is rich in figurative language, and so are most forms of descriptive writing.

THE NEXT GENERATION

11 In paragraph five of the article, the well-fed and sleeping baby is described as '7.90 kg of slumbering greed'.

What pictures enter your head when you read this phrase? Can you find any other phrases or images in the passage which suggest the ideas listed below? (The number of the paragraph in which the answer will be found is given.)

   a Helplessness   (4)
   b Falling movement (7)
   c Noise   (8)
   d Untidiness   (5)

Are these images metaphors or similes?

Make a list of five metaphors and five similes of your own which describe any qualities you like that are connected with babies or children.

12 You have probably already looked at the use of similes and metaphors in answering questions 9, 10 and 11, and decided whether you think they are effective or not. Now look at the following sonnet by Shakespeare. Throughout the sonnet there is the development of one metaphorical idea, but within that all-embracing idea there are other uses of figurative language. Explain the underlying metaphor, and then pick out examples of personification, metaphor and simile and decide how effective you think they are.

Sonnet 19

Devouring Time blunt thou the lion's paws,
And make the earth devour her own sweet brood,
Pluck the keen teeth from the fierce tiger's jaws,
And burn the long-lived phoenix in her blood,
Make glad and sorry seasons as thou fleet'st,   5
And do whate'er thou wilt swift-footed Time
To the wide world and all her fading sweets:
But I forbid thee one most heinous crime,
O carve not with thy hours my love's fair brow,
Nor draw no lines there with thine antique pen,   10
Him in thy course untainted do allow,
For beauty's pattern to succeeding men.
   Yet do thy worst old Time: despite thy wrong,
   My love shall in my verse ever live young.

William Shakespeare

15
STATING YOUR CASE

The two passages and the poem that follow are about prisons and imprisonment. The first passage is an article from 'The Observer' newspaper in which the journalist describes a visit to Wormwood Scrubs and asks what purpose prisons are supposed to serve. The second passage is a letter to a newspaper in which the writer, who spent a short time in prison, gives her impression of prison life. The poem by Hugh Lewin is for a South African imprisoned for life.

PEOPLE IN PRISON

A prison is still a prison, however much fresh primrose paint you slap on its rock-heavy walls. Walking round Wormwood Scrubs, one of Britain's biggest and the one where all life sentences start, it's at first hard to realise, though, that the thousand or so inmates are being held in there by force.

For the first impression is cheerful enough: men busy in workshops; prisoners trotting purposefully through the long corridors on errands; the casual ordinary rhythm of any large institution with its own ways, its own rules and its own times of day.

Only the high wire fences, and the dogs and the groups of warders watching the men in their blue denim uniforms walking round and round the windy exercise yard remind you that this is not, in fact, a barracks or a big boarding school. It is a prison so overcrowded that the men have to spend the greater part of every day locked in their cells. They must feel awful enough when there's no door-handle on the inside; but the cells of the lifers seem very much like my son's room, only tidier — same size, same posters; and one of them had a tame bird flying in and out of a cage.

STATING YOUR CASE

It is the sheer ordinariness of the prison that forces so insistently the question nobody answers: what is it all supposed to be for? The Victorians, who built the Scrubs as if it were a model fortress, had no doubts: a prison was for punishment. But that's now considered barbaric and ineffective. Is it there to reform the men? That was Elizabeth Fry's notion, to be accomplished with Bible readings and useful work; but in practice there's precious little of either. The Scrubs has a small therapeutic unit where those who opt for it get group therapy, five hours a day, remorselessly for months, but even when it works, that's just for a tiny minority.

To keep people off the streets, so they can't hurt anyone while they're inside? Not a bad idea – but then, the length of time you're inside ought to depend on how likely you are to do it again. So the persistent petty thief would be in for ever, and the man who had taken a once-for-all meat cleaver to a faithless wife would walk free. Perhaps the real answer is the one given by one of the larger and saner warders: he said simply 'to ease the conscience of society'; by shutting these men away, people can let themselves off worrying about why the crimes were committed.

Not that the prison people worry, either: the crime's the last thing they think about. This warder said he didn't even know the crimes of three-quarters of the men in his charge: there's even a sort of prison convention that you don't mention whatever it is the man's in for. This is the thing that is most amazing to the outsider. After the first few days, they all agree, the only thing that counts for the prisoner is making things as tolerable as possible – as it is for the warders, only from the opposite point of view. But if the crime's not important, what are they doing there at all?

All enlightened people concerned with prisons take the same line: perhaps they would find it intolerable, in their day-to-day dealings with these men, if they had to think 'He's the one who bashed up that old lady.' There are gaps, all the same, in the insistence on ignoring what got the men in there. Governor McCarthy, most humane of men, can't quite stomach drug pushers; bleeding-heart Tony Parker, who even put an appendix to his prison book suggesting that sexual assault doesn't really much harm children, confessed repugnance to, of all things, fraud; the prisoners themselves beat up those who have monkeyed around with little girls. But by and large, they're all to be treated equally; whether they are weak or wicked, impassioned or coldly sly – or just one of the vast number who are simply inadequate, the hapless people whose maunderings happened, this time, to have included something indictable.

The men are in prison because of a crime; yet the prison doesn't seem to relate to the crime in any way. It can't punish and reform at the same time; so in practice it doesn't do either. It is simply a parallel society, out of which, in due course, a man will emerge: maybe better, maybe worse; but probably much the same as before.

STATING YOUR CASE

Small wonder that concerned people more and more ask what on earth could be tried instead: they'll look at anything that seems to extend the range of the three standard options of fine, probation or prison. More money has just been voted for those who, since the 1972 Criminal Justice Act, can do community service; that's something. One or two judges in Germany have tried punishments that do seem to relate to the crime – making motorbike tearaways, for example, go to work in an accident ward; but of course half the time there isn't any such appropriate punishment available.

Martin Wright, for 10 years President of the Howard League for Penal Reform, has just got out a book called 'Making Good'. It's about the idea of making restitution to the victim, since the one thing a prison can never in any circumstances do is anything at all for the person the criminal has hurt. The snags facing reparation are horrendous, but there are several such schemes starting up; and they do have the blessing of some victims' organisations, offenders' organisations and even some of the police.

We buy crime books in their millions, we watch crime series on TV five times a night; we're obsessed with the idea of those who committed a crime being caught and brought to justice. But when that's all over we seem totally uninterested in what happens next. Put them away, shut them up, hide them; and we can forget all about them – until the next time when we can get indignant all over again.

Katharine Whitehorn

Suggested activities

1 From lines 1–16 write down:
 a the author's first impressions of the prison;
 b the things she sees which convince her that those first impressions are mistaken.

2
 a What, according to the author, did the Victorians think that prisons were for?
 b What purpose did Elizabeth Fry think that prisons should serve?

3 In lines 25–33 the author herself considers why we imprison people. Find two different reasons that she gives, and discuss them. Say why you think we imprison people.

4
 a What is the attitude of the warders to the crimes which the prisoners have committed?
 b Explain why you approve or disapprove of the attitude of the warders.

STATING YOUR CASE

5

a Explain what the author means by 'the three standard options of fine, probation or prison' (*line 62*)

b Study reports of court cases in a newspaper and notice what sentence is passed when someone is convicted. If you find a case where you disagree with the sentence, give the reasons why you disagree and say what you would have done had you been the judge or the magistrate.

6 Find out, from the passage, what alternative forms of punishment are being tried and say what you think of these alternatives.

Creative work

7 Imagine one of the following scenes carefully, forming a clear picture of each of the people involved. Make up a conversation which could take place.

a The convicted prisoner, escorted by a warder, has arrived at the prison. He/she is taken to the Governor's office.

b The prisoner is released and goes to the pub where his/her friends usually meet.

c The ex-prisoner is sorry for his/her crime and goes to visit the person who suffered from his/her actions.

8

a You are a Senior Warder at a prison and a trainee warder has been appointed to work with you. Write a report for the Prison Governor on the trainee's progress.

b The inmates of the prison give their opinion of the trainee. You may give the opinion of one man or woman, or you may summarise a number of opinions.

9 In the last paragraph (*lines 76–81*) the journalist says that most of us like reading crime stories or watching crime series on television.

a Work with a partner, and write down as many as you can remember of the crime stories you have read and the films you have seen on television or at the cinema. If possible, list them under different headings. These might be the different crimes dealt with in each story or film, but you should decide on your own means of classification.

b Using copies of the *Radio Times* and *TV Times*, count up the number of television programmes in one week that deal with crime. How many hours do they amount to?
   Discuss with your partner the factors that make crime stories and films dull or successful. Then choose one from your list, make brief notes about it and then expand your notes into a review, saying what was good about the book/film/programme and why you enjoyed it.

STATING YOUR CASE

In the passage you have just read, the author is looking at prisons from the outside. She is not herself a prisoner. In the letter and poem which follow we are given something of the prisoner's point of view.

The Editor
British Medical Journal
British Medical Association
Tavistock Square
LONDON   WC1

Dear Sir,

Before I went to prison (I served seven days in Holloway as a peace protester in March 1983) I imagined that the worst thing would be the claustrophobic conditions of confinement. And indeed, they are hard to endure: each cell, measuring 8 paces by 6 paces, is shared by three women; there is an open lavatory, with no privacy, no facilities for the disposal of sanitary towels, and very little ventilation; here women are locked in for as long as 20 hours a day, if there is a shortage of staff.

But this was not the worst thing; nor was it the food, although that was inedibly salty and over-cooked; nor was it the lack of exercise, although the only respite from confinement in tiny cells filled with tobacco smoke was 20 minutes spent walking round and round a yard each day; nor was it the mind-numbing boredom, although the only activity provided to fill the time is repetitive work such as putting paper hats in Christmas crackers, or assembling toy cars.

The worst thing was to witness the progressive mental deterioration of women isolated from their families, anxious about the welfare of their children, dependent for news of them on the whim of a prison officer, who might or might not produce the correct form which has to be filled in before a prisoner can have access to a telephone. I observed that the stress of separation often produces acute anxiety for the first few days, followed by deepening depression. In the long term, many women sentenced to imprisonment of six months or more display an apparent indifference to the welfare of their children, whom they may see for only half an hour a month, if at all. Such indifference, feigned or real, is one way of dealing with the pain.

Richard Smith is right to question whether prison has any success in rehabilitating women prisoners, and to ask (25 February, p.633) whether, 'because it plucks them out of their communities and families and separates them from their children, prison is more likely to aggravate the problems of both the women and their children'.

Yours faithfully,

Catherine M. Robinson

STATING YOUR CASE

10
- a What did the writer imagine would be the worst thing about being imprisoned *before* she went to the prison?
- b What did she consider the worst thing about being imprisoned *after* she had been to prison?

11 In your own words, explain the meaning of the following words and phrase as they are used in the letter:

- a the only respite from confinement (*line 11*)
- b mind-numbing boredom (*line 13*)
- c progressive mental deterioration (*line 16*)
- d whim (*line 18*)
- e apparent indifference (*line 23*)
- f rehabilitating (*line 28*)

12 In about 150 words summarise the writer's description and assessment of life in prison.

Another Day

It was like any other day
from un-lock
    breakfast/wash-up/scrub/clean
    garden/lunch
    lock-up   5
    wash-up/scrub/clean
    shower/4 o'clock supper
    lock-up
till un-lock next morning
any day every day   10
14 hour lock-up
every night

In the morning
we picked our 11 mielies*
10 for us 1 for the boer   15
which passed half an hour
and another half-hour passed
tearing off the husks
excited about our own-grown mielies
which we sent to be cooked for supper.   *20*

*Mielies = maize

STATING YOUR CASE

In the afternoon
we trimmed the 21 tomato bushes
and were pleased to see
how they were springing up
green with fruitfulness.   25

It was like any other day
 garden/lunch
 lock-up
 wash-up/scrub/clean
 shower/4 o'clock supper 30
but just before supper
he was called
unexpectedly
for a visit
which means I said   35
 either something good
 or something bad
So he missed supper with us
and we took his mielie to his cell
to eat after his visit   40
 either something good
 or something bad

It was like any other day
 supper/lock-up
 alone   45
 cell alone
 for 14 hours

While we ate
he was in the room
where you peer at your visitors 50
through a 4 inch strip of perspex
boxed in by wood panels
with sound-boards
to make the tapes clear.
You have boere on your side 55
they have boere on their side.
They call it the visitors room

His brother
peering through the perspex
into the wooden box   60
told him:

STATING YOUR CASE

>Your son died this morning.
>through the perspex
>into the wooden box
>keeping the State secure 65
>Your son died this morning.
>
>His supper I suppose was cold
>by the time he got back to his cell
> alone
>after lock-up 70
>for the next 14 hours
>like any other day.

Hugh Lewin

Further activities

13 What did the poem make you think about? Read the poem aloud. What impressions has the poet tried to give by his choice of words?

14 Pick out words or phrases which you find striking. Explain why you have chosen those particular words and phrases.

15

a What has (i) 'excited' them and (ii) 'pleased' them?

b How do you think that lines 19–25 are different from the lines that come before them and those that come immediately afterwards?

16 Working in small groups, improvise a play about being in prison. You may use some of the ideas from either of the passages or the poem, but you should try to show the boredom that all three mention. You may wish to include some or all of these events:

a One prisoner from a small group is suddenly taken away. Nobody knows why.

b A new prisoner is introduced to his/her cell mates.

c Prisoners are discussing the rumour that a terrorist who bombed a shopping precinct is to be put in the next door cell.

d An escape is being planned, and everyone wants to get out.

STATING YOUR CASE

Essays that express an opinion or argue a point of view

When you are asked to write or speak giving your opinion on some topic, you should try to give reasons for your opinions. A string of opinions or assertions, with no justification, is unconvincing.

None of the above passages sets out to argue a point of view or express an opinion, though each raises issues about which we might have a point of view of our own.

Suppose you are asked to write or speak on the topic: 'Children watch too much television'. Work through the following procedure.

a Write down the points which seem to favour watching television.

b Write down the points which seem to be against children watching it.

It may help if you arrange your lists in columns as shown.

For television watching	Against television watching
1. You learn things	1. You can waste a lot of time
2. It is entertaining	2. It encourages violence
3.	3. ....

c When you have made your lists, decide whether you are going to argue *for* or *against* the suggestion that children watch too much television. Then re-arrange the points in your lists so that they are in the order you want them to appear in your essay.

d In an essay you might give all the reasons *for* something and then all the reasons *against*. But you might find it more effective to take particular points in order and consider each point from all angles before passing on to the next. Each point will then be the basis of a paragraph.

e Decide on the approximate number of paragraphs and their order, then write an *Introductory* paragraph. This need only be two or three sentences long, but it should show the direction your essay is going to take.

f Now use the material you have organised in stage d to write the body of your essay.

g Write a concluding paragraph, in which you make clear your own opinion or point of view.

17 When you have worked through stages a–g, choose a topic for yourself about which people disagree, **or** choose a topic suggested by the passages and poem about prisons, such as 'A prison is for punishment'.

Plan the essay and then write it. You can write the essay *for* or *against* whatever proposition you choose.

16
SAYING GOODBYE

In the following story the author introduces us to the main characters and carefully places them against the background of their native countryside. When Derry leaves for America can you guess how the story will end?

THE GREEN HILLS

'What's the use of cryin'?' he asked.

'It makes your eyes sparkle,' she said.

'It also makes them red and ugly,' he said.

'Well, at least,' she said, 'they are my own eyes and I can do what I like with them.'

They were silent for a time.

They sat beneath the brow of the green hill. They could see below them and the silent sea out beyond as placid as a good dream. The red sun was just about to plunge into the sea. You'd almost listen to hear the sizzling sound it should make. That was on their right. And on their left the moon was in the sky, crescented, its light lit, ready with its feeble but fertile challenge to the departing sun. It was a warm evening. The bracken on which they sat was crinkly dry.

He was leaning back on his elbow, plucking at the fading blossoms of the heather, idly, tearing it with strong brown fingers.

'The village looks nice now from here,' he said.

It did. It was small. There were six houses, all newly built inside the last few years. Some of them were plastered with a white cement, some of them roughcast with a cream dash. They sat in a regular half-circle around the small quay. The school was in the middle. The priest came over from the other side to say Mass there on Sundays. It looked nice. You could see four currachs drawn up on the yellow sands and the mast of a hooker, rope festooned, rising from the far side of the quay. There was a dog barking in

SAYING GOODBYE

the street. They were high up on the hill. Over from them, around the shoulder of the hill, a mountain stream rushed down to seek the sea. It didn't rush much now. It wanted rain to make it roar. But you could hear it if you listened for it.

'It looks nice,' she said. 'I hope you will remember it.'

'I know it's nice,' he said. 'I will probably remember it. But there are bound to be places just as nice as it.'

'Do you mean that, now,' she asked, 'or are you only saying it because you're beginning to feel lonely already?'

Her back was towards him, her head bent. It was a good back, a good strong back, tapering to a narrow waist. Her hair, cut short for utility's sake, was brown with flecks of lighter hair bleached by the sun. He knew her face. It was broad and handsome, well shaped and firm. That was it – firm. Firm eyebrows and a small firm nose and chin with the lips turned out as if they were pursed. Her eyes were startlingly light blue and direct, but they could be soft.

'No,' he said, 'I'm not getting lonely already. I have been away before.'

'But this time you won't be coming back,' she said.

'I don't know,' he said. 'I might, but I hope I won't be coming back. I hope that if I come back I will come back with money in my pocket which I will spend freely and that I will go away again, and that this time you will come with me.'

'No,' she said.

'Why, but why?' he asked.

'We've said it all before,' she said. 'What's the use, Derry?'

'What the hell is there below there,' he asked with an impatient sweep of his arm, 'that binds you to it?'

'I just like it, that's all,' she said. 'That's all. I just like it. I like what we have and I don't think anywhere else could be the same as it, and I just like it, that's all.'

'How can you know?' he asked. 'How in the name of God can you know until you see other places to compare with it? Are you happy to spend your whole life here, growing old and dying and never to have been out of it?'

'I am,' she said.

'Well, I'm not,' he said decisively. 'You talk about the green hills. What green hills? You talk about green hills as if there weren't any green hills anywhere else in the world. There are. I saw them. I saw green hills that'd make this one look like it had the mange.' He got up and then stooped and took her hand and pulled her up to face him. He was tall: he looked down at her face. She looked at him. 'Didn't I tell you you'd make your eyes red? They are. Listen, Martha, there's just this difference between us. You want to stay here. I want to go away from it. That's the only difference. One of us will have to give way. We know what it means. What it will mean not to be

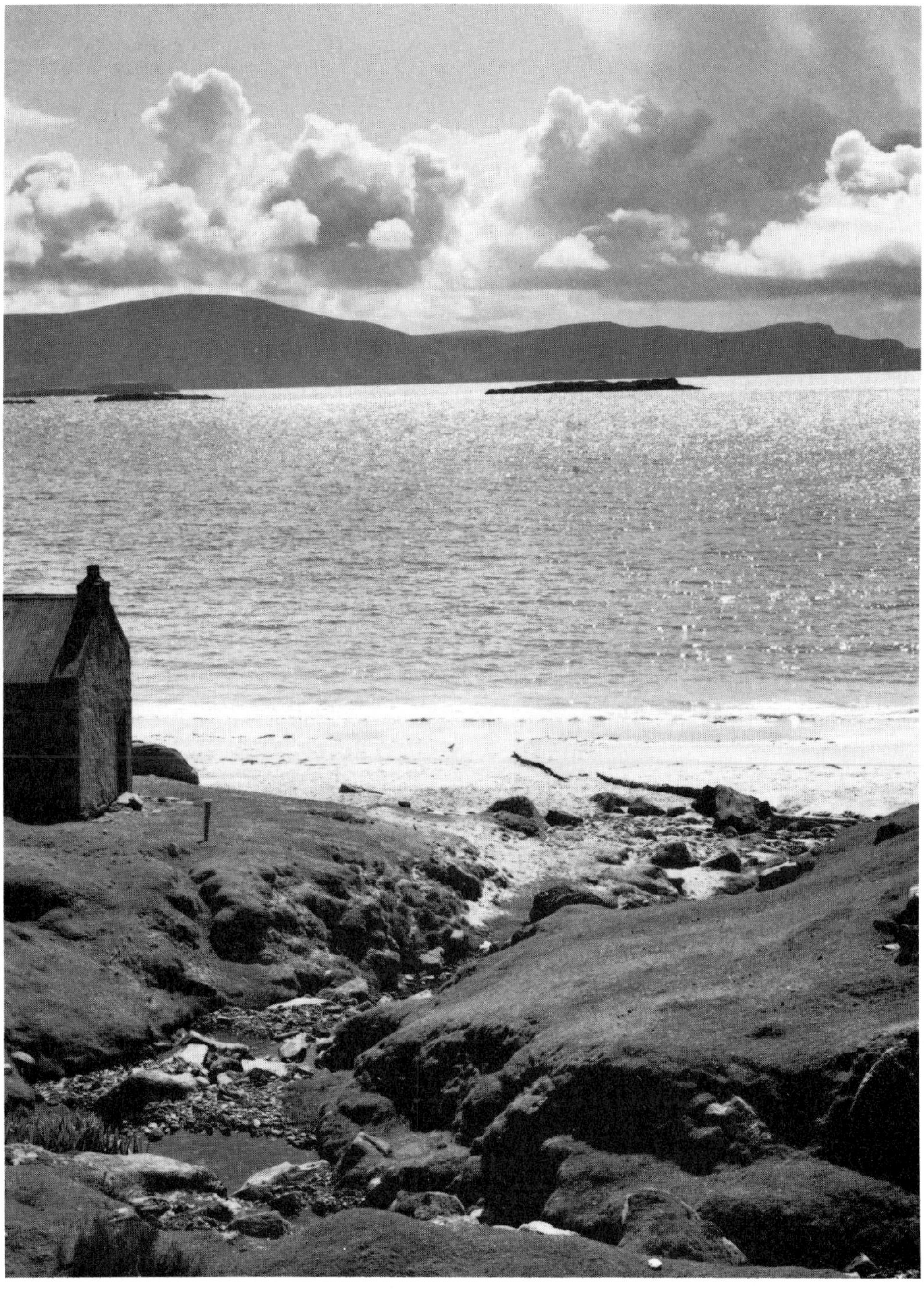

SAYING GOODBYE

together. I tell you when I come back for you you will forget the green hills.'

'There's more between us,' she said, looking into the restless eyes. 'You have shocking ambition. That's between us. Why can't you be ambitious here? Why do you have to go three thousand miles to be ambitious?'

'Here! What's here?' he asked, breaking away from her. 'Nothing. Work, work, work. What you get? You get enough to eat. New suit in a year, a bicycle on the hire purchase. Cycle ten miles to a picture. Six miles to a dance. Year in year out. Gloom in winter. Fish, shoot. But we're not getting anywhere. We're not just doing anything. I just can't stand it. You know what can happen. I'll get on. I'll get on fast. I have it up here. I'll become somebody. You'll see.'

'That's the trouble,' she said. 'I know you will, and I don't know that you'll be the better of it.' The broad shoulders, the close-cropped hair, the brown strong face and the restless eyes. Oh, he'd get somewhere all right. He was like a big city man at this moment with his well-cut double-breasted suit and the white shirt and light shoes looking incongruous on the side of a Connemara hill. He came back to her. He put his big arms around her. She could feel his breath on her face.

'You'll change, my girl,' he said. I could change in a minute, she thought, when I am as close to him as this. 'You can't whip our feeling. You'll see. I'm willing to put up with it until I come back for you. I'll make that gift to you, the fact that I have to come back to you, that I can't force you to come with me. You wait for me. You take up with any of the lads below and I'll murder them, you'll see. You hear that.'

'I do,' she said.

They heard his father's voice calling then. He was coming up the hill. He kissed her hard. Her lips were bruised against her teeth. But she strained to him. Almost his heart missed a beat, at the thought that he would be without her. But the restlessness came back to him. A four-engined plane winging over the sea with a gigantic continent below waiting to be conquered by Derry O'Flynn. It would be done. Lesser men had done it before him if they had the sluggish Irish blood that seemed to gush and gurgle with restless achievement once they got away from the inertia of their own villages.

'Goodbye, darling, for now,' said Derry.

'Goodbye,' she said, her head hiding in his chest.

'There you are,' his father said, coming up with the slow loping stride of the shepherd. The dog was with him. He was a big loose-limbed man. In the moonlight you could mistake him for his son if his eyes weren't so quiet. Then where did Derry get the eyes? His mother below was a quiet-eyed woman too.

'There's a few people in below now,' the father said. 'We better go down to the house.'

'I'll go down to them,' said Derry. 'Let ye come after me. I'll see ye below.'

SAYING GOODBYE

And he was gone, bounding down the hill like a goat, sideways and forward and jumping and never missing a step. They stood and watched him become smaller and smaller.

'He has a lot of energy,' said Derry's father.

'He has a lot of ambition,' said Martha, moving off. He looked after her. She was probably crying, he thought. He knew Derry's mother was crying. He wondered idly if the tears of women would make a big river, all the tears of all the women in the world. What good did all those tears do ever? Did they ever soften a heart or deflect a man from a purpose; or if they did, what did their success mean but frustration afterwards? He sighed and caught up with her.

'Going to America is not what it was when I was young,' he said as he walked beside her. He admired Martha very much. She could walk down a hill like a healthy sheep.

'It's different,' she said.

'Man,' he said, 'if you were going to America when I was young, you'd have to be preparing for a year. Everyone within fifty miles knew you were going, and they'd all make sure to see you before you left and wish you away with a tear or a little gift or a holy medal to guard you from the perils of the deep or a good scapular. Now – well, look at it now.'

'It's been pepped up,' said Martha, smiling. 'Isn't it only twelve hours away? It's quicker now to go there than to go to Dublin.'

'Spoiled they have it,' he said. 'Man, we used to have great times at the wakes before they went. We'd all cry our eyes out and we'd dance and drink porter until the small hours of the mornin'. I suppose you can't feel sorry for people now when they're only twelve hours away. Sure they could be only in the next parish.'

'You'll miss Derry,' she said.

He faltered then, of course.

'Oh, not much,' he said. 'It's like I'm saying. You haven't time. It's not the same. Besides, Derry was always restless. This is his third time away. Twice before, he was in England. He was always a restless one. I don't know where we got him. Sometimes I say to his mother that she must have been courted by a wandering one on the sly.' He chuckled at this. 'You should have gone with him, Martha,' he said then, gently. 'He's very set on you.'

'I'm set on him too,' she said. 'But I'm set on here. I think he should be ambitious at home. It would take little to make me go with him, but it will be better that I don't.'

'I know him,' said his father. 'He will come back for you.'

'Maybe by then,' she said, 'I will have changed, or he will have changed. Let him have his head now, and he will conquer the green hills of America.'

'Will you come into the house?' he asked as they paused on the street. 'A few of his friends and a few bottles of stout and a few songs. Man, but it's

SAYING GOODBYE

only a ghost of the good wakes long ago.'

'I'll go home,' she said. 'We've said all that's to be said. I will see him when he comes home.'

'All right. Good night, girl. God bless you.'

He watched her away. She walked slowly, her head was bent. One hand was behind her holding her other arm. She was idly kicking small stones out of her way. He sighed and turned towards the door of his house. There was no noise coming from it. Somehow this annoyed him. He spoke out loud. 'Man, years ago the roof would have been coming off that house with the noise,' he said. He went in.

Derry came back for her. Almost a year to the day. But he didn't come alone. He was accompanied by two American sergeants and a firing party of American soldiers, and he had an American flag on his coffin, and his father had a medal that was given to Derry for bravery in some foreign war, and he was planted in the small graveyard halfway up the green hill, right beside the stream that roared when the rain hit the hill and tinkled when it was low. And from here if you stood by his grave to put fresh flowers in the glass jar, you could look out across the wide expanse of the sea; and if you had the vision, miles and miles away you could see the green hills on the other side of the world.

Walter Macken

Suggested activities

1 The title of the story suggests that it is to be about a place, but it starts with a conversation between two people. Do you think this is a good way to begin a story like this? Discuss with a partner, or in a small group, whether you think the story is mostly about the Green Hills in the title, about saying goodbye, or about the people who appear in the story.

2 From *the first six lines of the story*, what impression do you get of the people who are speaking?

3 Derry and Martha are in love, but Derry is going away to America without Martha because she will not leave the Green Hills to accompany him.

a What reasons does Derry give to Martha for going away?

b Derry's father suggests other reasons. Why does his father think that Derry is going away?

SAYING GOODBYE

4 After the first six lines of conversation which you considered for question 2, the narrator (the person telling the story) comes in and tells us about the place where the two people live.

a What impression of the place does the narrator try to give us in lines 6–27? (You might find it helpful to look at the passage about Kettlewell on page 46.)

b Write down from these lines two phrases or sentences about the village, and two about the countryside, in which the writer suggests beauty and peacefulness. Why did you choose these lines?

5 We sometimes talk about people being attached to their roots when we mean that people feel a deep attachment to the place where they were born or in which they were brought up. Martha has this sort of attachment. Think about why people might feel this attachment, and then

either
a Explain how you might act and feel if you had the chance of leaving home and the place in which you have always lived. Would your reactions be more like Derry's or Martha's?

or
b You may long to leave your 'roots', and wish to live elsewhere. Describe where you would prefer to live and why. Might you regret your decision?

6 The following phrases or sentences each suggest something about the character referred to. Find each phrase or sentence in the story and say what you think is suggested about the character referred to.

a Her hair, cut short for utility's sake, was brown with flecks of lighter hair bleached by the sun. (*lines 34–5*)

b . . . he asked with an impatient sweep of his arm (*lines 49–50*)

c The broad shoulders, the close-cropped hair, the brown strong face and the restless eyes. (*lines 79–80*)

d I could change in a minute, she thought, when I am as close to him as this. (*lines 85–6*)

e lesser men had done it before him (*line 97*)

f In the moonlight you could mistake him for his son if his eyes weren't so quiet. (*lines 103–4*)

g He admired Martha very much. She could walk down a hill like a healthy sheep. (*lines 122–3*)

h He sighed and turned towards the door of his house. (*line 159*)

SAYING GOODBYE

7 Make up, and either act out or tape record, one of the following conversations:

a The conversation which Derry had with his father on the morning of the day he left for America.

b A conversation which Martha and Derry's father might have on meeting on the hills some time after the return and burial of Derry.

8 The story takes place on the west coast of Ireland.

a What do you think a *wake* is, as the word is used in this story? (See for example, line 133.)

b Why do you think Derry's father regrets that wakes are not as good as they used to be?

9 In lines 71–7 Derry gets very excited. How do you think the words the author uses and the way he uses them suggest Derry's excitement and agitation?

10 The author repeats some words quite often; 'restless', 'nice' and 'green' are three of them. Make a note of where he uses these words and discuss the effect made by them. Is the author deliberately repeating himself? Would other words have been more suitable?

11 The last paragraph of the story gives us an unexpected ending. Derry does come home to the Green Hills, but not in the way we expected.

a Explain why you think the ending of the story is, or is not, a good one.

b Re-write the ending of the story so that it is a happy one.

c Do you prefer your ending or the ending given by the author? Give reasons for your preference.

12 Explain

either

why you think Martha was right not to go with Derry

or

why you think she should have gone with him.

What would you have done?

SAYING GOODBYE

Edward Thomas, who wrote the following poem, was killed in action in Flanders in 1917, at the age of thirty-nine. He had established a reputation as a writer before 1914; he need not have gone to the war, because of his age, but he never turned back from his decision. In this poem, the poet is on leave from the fighting in France, and we are shown the rural life he loved and would soon have to leave again. The poem describes the ploughing of a field with a team of horses pulling the plough, and gives bits of conversation between the ploughman and the poet.

   Note: the head-brass is part of the horse's harness, and the share (line 10) is a ploughshare. Charlock (line 6) is a plant, field mustard, which has a yellow flower.

·AS THE TEAM'S HEAD BRASS·

As the team's head-brass flashed out on the turn
The lovers disappeared into the wood.
I sat among the boughs of the fallen elm
That strewed the angle of the fallow, and
Watched the plough narrowing a yellow square   5
Of charlock. Every time the horses turned
Instead of treading me down, the ploughman leaned
Upon the handles to say or ask a word,
About the weather, next about the war.
Scraping the share he faced towards the wood,   10
And screwed along the furrow till the brass flashed
Once more.
            The blizzard felled the elm whose crest
I sat in, by a woodpecker's round hole,
The ploughman said. 'When will they take it away?' 15
'When the war's over.' So the talk began –
One minute and an interval of ten,
A minute more and the same interval.
'Have you been out?' 'No.' 'And don't want to,
      perhaps?'
'If I could only come back again, I should.   20
I could spare an arm. I shouldn't want to lose

SAYING GOODBYE

A leg. If I should lose my head, why, so,
I should want nothing more. . . . Have many gone
From here?' 'Yes.' 'Many lost?' 'Yes, a good few.
Only two teams work on the farm this year. 25
One of my mates is dead. The second day
In France they killed him. It was back in March,
The very night of the blizzard, too. Now if
He had stayed here we should have moved the tree.'
'And I should not have sat here. Everything 30
Would have been different. For it would have been
Another world.' 'Ay, and a better, though
If we could see all all might seem good.' Then
The lovers came out of the wood again:
The horses started and for the last time 35
I watched the clods crumble and topple over
After the ploughshare and the stumbling team.

Edward Thomas

Further activities

13 When you have read and understood the poem, discuss your impression of it with a partner. Look carefully at the way in which it is written and find where the following 'themes' are placed:

a a team of horses pulling a plough;
b conversation between the poet and the ploughman;
c the poet's own thoughts.

Are there any lines or ideas that do not seem to fit into any of these categories?

14 Having read lines 1–18, describe the scene as fully as you can and explain what is happening.

15

a What do you think is the significance of

'One minute and an interval of ten' (line 17)?

b Why do you think the poet chooses to stress this detail?

Remembering that the poet has soon got to return to the war, explain what you understand by:

c 'Have you been out?' (line 19).

d 'If I could only come back again, I should.
I could spare an arm. I shouldn't want to lose
A leg . . . (lines 20–22).

SAYING GOODBYE

16 Why do you think the poet mentions the lovers in lines 2 and 34? What do they suggest to you and how does his mentioning them contrast with his thoughts about returning to the war?

17 Note down the occasions when the poet refers to the fallen elm tree. How does he link these references to his thoughts about the war?

18 Look at the last three lines of the poem. What do you think the poet's thoughts might have been when he wrote these lines?

19 either
Imagine that you are involved in fighting in a war in a foreign country. Write a letter home to someone you love telling him or her what is happening and sharing your thoughts and feelings about the place where you lived and which you may never see again.

or
Write a letter to someone you love or who is a close friend of yours who is fighting abroad. You may particularly wish to remind him or her of the beauties of the place where you both lived and what is happening there.

20 Write imaginatively, in any way you like, on a topic suggested by the following poem.

In Memoriam (Easter, 1915)

The flowers left thick at nightfall in the wood
This Eastertide call into mind the men,
Now far from home, who, with their sweethearts, should
Have gathered them and will do never again.

Edward Thomas

17
A SENSE OF PLACE

The following poem and newspaper article are about changes which have taken place in city areas: the poem is set in Leeds and the article is about the East End of London. One shows the poet's personal view, and the other gives more information about change.

LEEDS 2

Houses once grand now condemned,
Gardens decayed to a playground
For ragged children, trees dirty
To touch are lit every morning
By the indirect sun; mist gathers   5
Here disclosing only green and brightness
And the everywhere elegant lines
Of trees and rooftops against the air.
Rubbish on grass doesn't offend
Then, nor could I wish for any other   10
Environment, nor anything lovelier
Than five minutes of standing
In the bare hall where door ajar
And grimed fanlight frame the garden;
Reversing the dutch painter's view   15
Also in my house-pride being perverse.
At mid-day lying on the grass
The hard ground and dung smells
And flung away bottles constrict
The place to a poor bit of nature,   20
Only better than a concrete yard;
But evening or snow, or rain

A SENSE OF PLACE

Adds the glow of emotion, sets off
Vague notions of regret for this
Victim of time the coming people   25
Will clear away. This old square
Is dying late. The people who lived
Here by choice have all left,
And through what used to be a gate
Come students, labourers and refugees   30
For temporary shelter from the traffic,
Audible all night like threatening seas
Beyond the private garden and the trees.

James Simmons

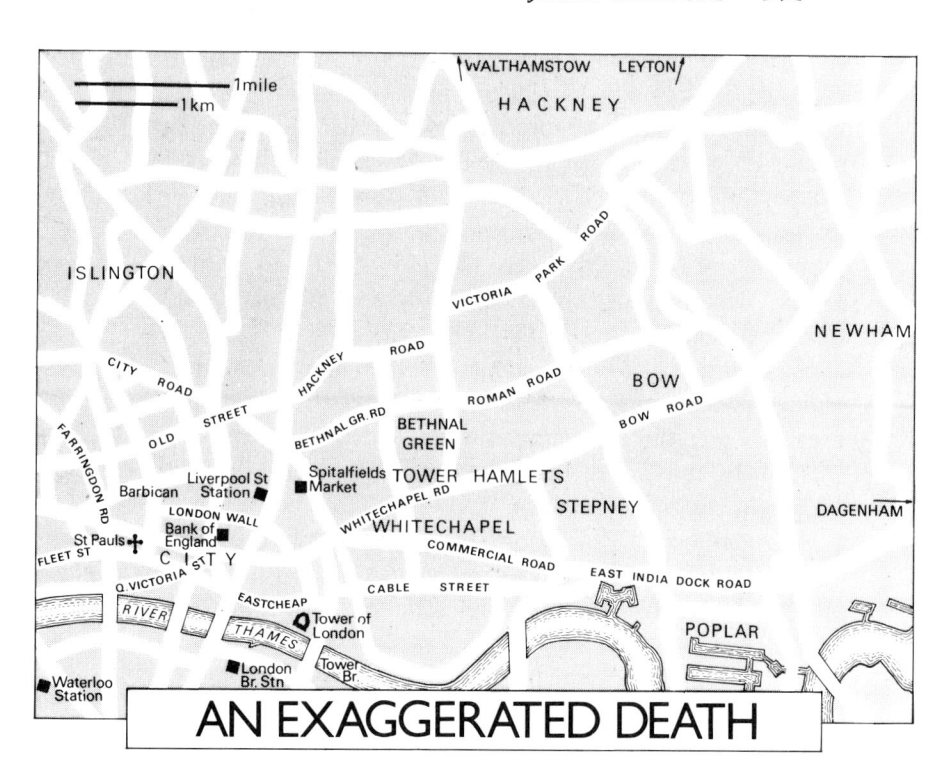

AN EXAGGERATED DEATH

An hour before dawn in Spitalfields Market, the air is heavy with scent of fruit, veg, flowers and diesel. Heavy lorries, bantamweight vans, and forklift trucks jostle for space. The sawdusty caffs dispense sausage butties and cheer, and the 300-year-old market heaves with life and humour.

On one side, the City of London lies silent, a shiny new cube of office space, nearly all glass in glittering white frames, opulently overlooking the rattling, old-fashioned porters' barrows.

A SENSE OF PLACE

On the market's opposite flank, the soaring bulk of Hawksmoor's Christ Church, on Commercial Street, guards the approaches to another London. The Church ground has been the refuge for centuries for tramps who use it to dream and booze and scratch. It is called, therefore, Itchy Park, and the East End starts here.

Where it ends is a puzzle. There are as many opinions on the matter as there are informants. Some say that the East End is Bethnal Green, Stepney, Whitechapel, Poplar, and Bow. Others say you have to include the boroughs of Hackney to the north, and Newham in the middle east. And there are those who say, extravagantly, that the East End has spread its spirit even wider, to Leyton, Walthamstow, Dagenham, Harlow, yea, even unto Southend.

The outsider seeking the East End is thus posed a pretty problem: Should the search take place on the streets or in the reference libraries? Is it a place at all, or a state of mind? The tentative answer, from this outsider, is that the death of the East End has been much exaggerated.

It survives, demonstrably, in the surprisingly large legacy of pre-war buildings, some of them almost handsome amid the encircling blight. It is still possible to extract a vicarious thrill from the alleys where Jack the Ripper ripped and Dickens rambled, to pay respects to the nondescript assembly rooms where Marat spoke, the hostel where Stalin and Litvinoff slept, the pretty Trinity House almshouses for ancient mariners, and the fading Georgian remains of a gentry long vanished.

Bill Fishman, who is Jewish and Leftish, is passionately devoted to the radical history of the East End. Rudolf Rocker, the anarchist tractarian, is his greatest hero, among many, and Oswald Mosley, his greatest villain. He was at the Cable Street confrontation in 1936 when the East Enders repelled Mosley's fascist black-shirts.

A gigantic new Salvation Army Hostel, Booth House, adjoins the original, still open, Victorian Home for Men in Whitechapel, and at both, most hours of the day, there are little knots of ragged down and outers waiting for food and shelter.

The new affluence, which dispersed the Jews of the East End, as yet eludes the newer communities which have made the place their home. The old pattern of immigration which filtered newcomers from the docks northwards to the more prosperous suburbs has been distorted by the death of Dockland. Tower Hamlets still has a huge collection of Yiddish books in its libraries, now hardly used, while Hackney, catering for second and third generation Jewish immigrants has very few. But the old instinct of linguistic groups to congregate persists. In Hackney, where the borough libraries have books in 21 languages, Turkish is now the second tongue in the schools. A couple of years ago, there were 35 Turkish books available, and 30 Greek. There are now several thousand of each: eight per cent of the population is reckoned to be Cypriot. Another 17 per cent of Hackney people are now Afro-Caribbean; approaching seven per cent are Asian.

Stan Newens, one of the very few genuine East Enders in the House of Commons, attributes the continuing plight of the district to the tendency of the better off and the better educated to move out, leaving behind the old and the disadvantaged and the new immigrants.

'After the war it was clear that there would have to be a big housing programme, and that it couldn't be in East London where there just wasn't enough room. But the great mistake was to build flats. What people wanted – East London people have always wanted them – was houses with gardens; that was the great tradition.

'One of the ways to get them was to move to the new towns when they were established after the war. To get a house you had to have a job, so after the initial wave for building workers the opportunities were restricted to people with skills,' he said.

Newens, now resident in Harlow, his constituency, is of course part of that selective exodus. His grandfather, a policeman, was drafted into the East End in 1888 in the panicky aftermath of the Ripper murders; now his sizeable family are dispersed all over the south-east of England and beyond, with a few relatives left in the East End.

Newens is anxious that this observation should not be construed as a criticism of the people who stayed behind, or the new people who have moved in. He is as proud of the East End as anybody; proud of his voice; his morally strictish upbringing with its stress on hard work and self-improvement.

The older parts of the East End were and remain dominated by small workshops and craftsmen. Huguenot silk weavers, Victorian cabinet makers, Jewish tailors, and Bengali dressmakers are all part of the same precariously independent tradition.

In a more general sense, the concern with establishing roots has taken flower with an explosion of interest in local history and genealogy. The East of London Family History Society has 600 members busily constructing family trees for themselves and for a regular stream of inquirers from around the world.

At one of the monthly workshop sessions of society members, Mrs Joyce McQueen proudly unleashed a family tree of around 700 names, going back to 1618 and covering about 15 feet of a roll of lining paper.

'My family were in Bethnal Green and Stepney for 200 years. My children laughed at me when I started all this. They said what do you expect to find, with a background like that. But I said to myself, I've come from somewhere, I must have ancestors like everyone else,' she said.

David Webb, chairman of the workshop group, gets frequent pleas for help from America, Australia, and other common destinations for

A SENSE OF PLACE

emigrant East Enders.

'There is great pride in this part of London. Many Americans in particular are thrilled to find they have roots here. I think now there is probably a cachet in having an East End ancestor,' he said.

The same pride and interest is reflected in the impressive surge of community publishing in the East of London, which started in the early seventies. Centerprise in Hackney runs a coffee shop, bookshop, advice service, and educational class as well as being a lively publishing concern. It has put out more than 40 books in the last ten years, including reminiscences, poetry, photographic records and histories, all produced by local people. The Centerprise Trust exists to promote the right of the local community to self-expression.

In the Crown pub in Redchurch Street, round the corner from Arthur Harding's first pigsty of a home, the bird fanciers of the area used to hang their cages on nails in the wall of a Sunday lunchtime. Now the pub is closed at weekends, and during the week it has nightly strip shows mainly for lorry drivers passing through.

Behind the bar, Jean Gilbert says how much she likes the local ways and local folk, though it's a shame what's happened to the pub. Her daughter Sandie, who's 18, says she feels totally safe in what used to be the Jago, and adds confusingly, that it's 'evil sometimes – you know, *hard*'. She can't wait to move out but has no job and therefore no opportunity.

In the Church of England primary school in Brick Lane, where the teachers once had to learn Yiddish before they could teach at all, the Way In sign is now translated helpfully into Bengali. Around the corner in Spitalfields, Renee, a Yiddish-speaking Polish Jewess, now 76, stands at the stall where she has worked for 53 years, humping boxes of fruit and veg. Over the road in Itchy Park, the winos stir in the dawn light. The signs of change are all around, but sometimes they are imperceptible.

Derek Brown

Suggested activities

1 Discuss with a partner or in a small group, the impression you got of the places described in the poem and the article.

2 Still working with a partner, think carefully about the ways in which the two writers deal with a similar subject. Draw up two columns on a large sheet of paper and note down the similarities and differences between the poem and the article.

3 What differences do you think there are between the attitude of the poet and the writer of the article to the subject of the changing inner-city areas?

A SENSE OF PLACE

Activities on the poem

4 With close reference to the actual words of the poem, say how the poet:

a Suggests that the area is in a state of decay.

b Gives the feeling that he himself is sorry that the houses are to be demolished and the area re-developed.

c Contrasts the people who used to live in these houses with those who are living there now.

5 Explain why the appearance of the area seems different in the early morning from how it appears at mid-day.

Activities on the newspaper article

6 Explain why:

a 'The outsider seeking the East End is thus posed a pretty problem' (*line 20*)

b the writer feels that the 'death of the East End has been much exaggerated' (*line 23*)

7 Stan Newens, the MP mentioned in line 53, gives one reason for 'the continuing plight of the district'. (*line 54*)
Explain the reason in your own words.

8 According to the writer, many people from the East End are finding out about their family histories, and are proud of belonging to East London.

a Find examples from the passage which show that people do take a pride in the area.

b Find out as much as you can about your own family history, and see how far back in time you can draw up a family tree.

Further work

9 Someone from the council housing department comes to tell an elderly couple who have lived in such an area all their lives that they are to be moved out into a flat some miles away. Make up the conversation between the three people. You may introduce other characters if you wish. (You may find it helpful to look back at page 44, at the notes on setting out conversation.)

10 Imagine that you have lived in such an area for the first twenty years of your life, but moved out a few years ago.

either

a Describe what your feelings are about the move and what you think have been the effects of the move, what have been the good things about it and what have been the bad.

or

b Write a letter to the local newspaper recalling your memories of the area.

A SENSE OF PLACE

11 Write one of the following essays:

 a   The advantages and disadvantages of living where you live. Explain why you would or would not recommend to anyone else that they should come and live there.

 b   Imagine that you are a refugee from a foreign country who has recently arrived in Leeds or the East End of London. Describe your experiences.

12 Look carefully at these two pictures of High Street, Sheffield, one taken in 1906 and the other more recently.

 a   Find as many differences as you can between the pictures.

 b   Try to find old pictures of the area in which you live. What changes have taken place?

A SENSE OF PLACE

Both the poem and the passage you have just read are about the ways in which particular places have changed. In both cases there is a sense of regret that this is so.

In the following poem it is not the place that has changed but the poet himself. He returns to a seaside he visited often as a child. The place itself and what happens there seem to be much as he remembers them. Yet his response appears to be very different from his response when he first went there. Perhaps he has some regrets that he has changed.

To the Sea

To step over the low wall that divides
Road from concrete walk above the shore
Brings sharply back something known long before –
The miniature gaiety of seasides.
Everything crowds under the low horizon: 5
Steep beach, blue water, towels, red bathing caps,
The small hushed waves' repeated fresh collapse
Up the warm yellow sand, and further off
A white steamer stuck in the afternoon –

A SENSE OF PLACE

Still going on, all of it, still going on! 10
To lie, eat, sleep in hearing of the surf
(Ears to transistors, that sound tame enough
Under the sky), or gently up and down
Lead the uncertain children, frilled in white
And grasping at enormous air, or wheel 15
The rigid old along for them to feel
A final summer, plainly still occurs
As half an annual pleasure, half a rite,

As when, happy at being on my own,
I searched the sand for Famous Cricketers, 20
Or, farther back, my parents, listeners
To the same seaside quack, first became known.
Strange to it, now, I watch the cloudless scene:
The same clear water over smoothed pebbles,
The distant bathers' weak protesting trebles 25
Down at its edge, and then the cheap cigars,
The chocolate-papers, tea-leaves, and, between

The rocks, the rusting soup-tins, till the first
Few families start the trek back to the cars.
The white steamer has gone. Like breathed-on glass 30
The sunlight has turned milky. If the worst
Of flawless weather is our falling short,
It may be that through habit these do best,
Coming to water clumsily undressed
Yearly; teaching their children by a sort 35
Of clowning; helping the old, too, as they ought.

Philip Larkin

Further activities

13 Working with a partner, go through the poem carefully and make a list of the activities that are going on.
   Discuss and write down the impression you get from reading the poem. Does it make you feel happy or sad or neither? Explain why you feel about it as you do, referring to details in the poem.

A SENSE OF PLACE

14 Explain as fully as you can the meaning of the following words in italics.

a Brings *sharply* back something known long before (*line 3*)
b The *miniature* gaiety of seasides (*line 4*)
c Wheel the rigid old along for them to feel
   A *final* summer (*lines 15–17*)
d As half an annual pleasure, half a *rite* (*lines 18*)
e ... my parents, listeners
   To the same seaside *quack*, first became known (*lines 21–2*)
f *Strange* to it now, I watch the cloudless scene (*line 23*)
g The *distant* bathers' weak protesting trebles (*line 25*)

15 Suggest in any way you like how you think the poet's attitude *now* is different from what it was when he first visited the place as a small boy. You should refer to or quote from the poem if it will help make clearer what you think the essential differences are.

16 Write down anything you notice about the pattern of the rhymes in the poem and give examples of where you think the impact or effectiveness of the poem is increased by the rhymes. Explain in each case how you think the rhyme adds to the effectiveness.

18
OVERSTEPPING THE LIMIT

♦

This story is not only about a man's relationship with a horse and with himself, but also perhaps about the powerful, instinctive, and inscrutable forces which seem to be close to him in the countryside where he lives.
You will find it helpful if you can read the story aloud.

·THE·BLACK·MARE·

I bought the mare at G——, from a red-whiskered tinker, and, if the truth were only known, I believe he stole her from somewhere in the south, for he parted with her for thirty shillings. Or else it was because she was so wild that there was not another man at the whole fair had the courage to cross her back with his legs and trot her down the fair green but myself, for it was not for nothing that they called me Dan of the Fury in those days. However, when I landed from the hooker at the pier at Kilmurrage and, mounting her, trotted up to the village, they all laughed at me. For she was a poor-looking animal that day, with long shaggy hair under her belly, and the flesh on her ribs was as scarce as hospitality in a priest's house. She didn't stand an inch over fourteen hands, and my legs almost touched the ground astride of her. So they laughed at me, but I paid no heed to them. I saw the fire in her eyes, and that was all I needed. You see this drop of whisky in this glass, stranger? It is a pale, weak colour, and it would not cover an inch with wetness, but it has more fire in it than a whole teeming lake of soft water. So the mare.

I set her to pasture in a little field I had between two hills in the valley below the fort. I cared for her as a mother might care for an only child, and all that winter I never put a halter in her mouth or threw my legs across her back, but I used to watch her for hours galloping around the fields snorting,

OVERSTEPPING THE LIMIT

with her great black eyes spitting fire and her nostrils opened so wide that you could hide an egg in each of them. And Virgin of the Valiant Deeds, when she shed her winter coat in spring and I combed her glossy sides, what a horse she was! As black as the sloes they pick on the slope of Coillnamhan Fort, with never a hair of red or white or yellow. Her tail swept to the ground, and when the sun shone on her sides you could see them shimmering like the jewels on a priest's vestments; may the good God forgive me, a sinner, for the comparison. But what is nearer to God than a beautiful horse? Tell me that stranger, who have been in many lands across the sea.

And then the day came when all the unbroken mares of Inverara were to be shod. For it was the custom then, stranger, to shoe all the young mares on the same day, and to break them before they were shod on the wide sandy beach beneath the village of Coillnamhan.

There were seven mares that day gathered together from the four villages of Inverara, and there were good horses among them, but none as good as mine. She was not a little over fifteen hands high, and you could bury a child's hand between her haunches. She was perfect in every limb, like a horse from the stable of the God Crom. I can see her yet, stranger, standing on the strand stamping with her hind leg and cocking her ears at every sound. But it's an old saying, talk of beauty to-day, talk of death to-morrow.

I kept her to the last, and gave her to a lad to hold while I mounted a bay mare that my cousin had brought from Kilmillick, and I broke her in three rounds of the strand, although she had thrown three strong and hardy men before I seized her halter. And then my mare was brought down, and then and there I offered three quarts of the best whisky that could be bought for money to the man that could stay on her back for one length of the strand. One after the other they mounted her, but no sooner did they touch her back than she sent them headlong to the ground. She would gather her four legs together and jump her own height from the ground, and with each jump they flew from her back, and she would run shivering around again until they caught her. I smiled, sitting there on the rock.

Then Shemus, the son of Crooked Michael, spat on his hands, tightened his crios around his waist, and said that if the devil were hiding in her bowels and Lucifer's own stepbrother riding on her mane, he would break her. He was a man I never liked, that same son of Crooked Michael, a braggart without any good in him, a man who must have come crooked from his mother's womb, and his father before him was the same dishonest son of a horse-stealing tinker. 'Be careful,' I said to him; 'that mare is used to have men about her that didn't drink their mother's milk from a teapot.' And when I saw the ugly look he gave me I knew that there was trouble coming, and so there was.

He got up on her all right, for, to give the devil his due, he was agile on his

OVERSTEPPING THE LIMIT

limbs and, although no horseman, there were few men in the island of Inverara that he coudn't throw with a twist of the wrist he had. But as soon as his legs rubbed her flanks she neighed and gathered herself together to spring, and just as she was that way doubled up he kicked her in the mouth with his foot. She rose to her hind legs and before she could plant her forefeet on the ground again to jump, I had rushed from the rock and with one swing of my right arm I had pulled him to the ground. I was so mad that before he could rush at me I seized him by the thigh and the back of the neck, and I would have broken every limb in his putrid body if they didn't rush in and separate us. Then, the craven son of a reptile that he was, as soon as he saw himself held, he began to bellow like a young bull wanting to get at me. But I took no heed of him. My father's son was never a man to crow over a fallen enemy.

They brought the mare over to me and I looked at her. She looked at me and a shiver passed down her flank, and she whinnied, pawing the sand with her hind hoof.

'Take off that halter,' said I to the men.

They did. I still kept looking at the mare and she at me. She never moved. Then coming over to her as she stood there without saddle or bridle, stepping lightly on my toes, I laid my right hand on her shoulder. 'Pruach, pruach, my beautiful girl,' I called to her, rubbing her shoulders with my left hand. Then I rose from the strand, leaning on the strength of my right hand, and landed on her back as lightly as a bird landing on a rose bush. She darted forward like a flash of lightning from a darkened sky. You see that strand, stretching from the rock to where it ends in a line of boulders at the eastern end? It is four hundred paces and it rises to the south of the boulders into a high sand-bank underneath the road. Well, I turned her at the sand-bank with a sudden flash of my hand across her eyes, leaning out over her mane. And then back again we came, with a column of sand rising after us and the ground rising up in front of us with the speed of our progress. 'Now,' said I to myself, 'I will show this son of Crooked Michael what Dan of the Fury can do on horseback.'

Raising myself gently with my hands on her shoulders, I put my two feet square on her haunches and stood straight, leaning against the wind, balancing myself with every motion of her body, and as she ran, stretched flat with her belly to earth, I took my blue woollen shirt off my back and was down again on her shoulders as light as a feather before we reached the western end, where the men stood gaping as if they had seen a priest performing a miracle. 'God be with a man!' they cried. And the women sitting on the hillock that overlooks the beach screamed with fear and enjoyment, and of all the beautiful women that were gathered there that day there was not one that would not have been glad to mate with me with or without marriage.

OVERSTEPPING THE LIMIT

Back over the strand again we went, the black mare and I, like lightning flying from the thunder and the wave that rose when we passed the rock in the west had not broken on the strand when we turned again at the sandbank. Then coming back again like the driven wind in winter I rose once more, standing on her haunches, and may the devil swallow me alive if I hadn't put my shirt on my back again and landed back on her shoulders before we reached the rock. There I turned her head to sea and drove her out into it until the waves lapped her heaving belly. I brought her back to the rock as gentle as a lamb and dismounted.

Ha! My soul from the devil, but that was a day that will never be forgotten as long as there is a man left to breathe the name of Dan of the Fury. But all things have their end, and sure it's a queer day that doesn't bring the night, and the laugh is the herald of the sigh. It was two years after that I got this fractured thigh. Well I remember that four days before the races where I got this broken limb, I met red-haired Mary of Kilmillick. As I was looking after her, for she had shapely hips and an enticing swing to them, my horse stumbled, and although I crossed myself three times and promised to make a journey to the Holy Well at Kilmillick, I'll swear by Crom that the spell of the Evil One was put on the mare. But that is old woman's talk. Mary promised me the morning of the races that if the black mare won I could put a ring on her finger, and as I cantered up to the starting-point I swore I would win both the race and the girl if the devil himself were holding on to the black mare's tail.

Seventeen horses lined up at the starting-point. I took up my position beside a bay stallion that the parish priest, Fr John Costigan, had entered. He was a blood stallion and had won many races on the mainland, but the parish priest was allowed to enter him, for who could go against a priest? Then, as now, there was nobody in Inverara who was willing to risk being turned into a goat by making a priest obey the rules of the race. Six times they started us and six times we were forced to come back to the starting-point, for that same braggart, the son of Crooked Michael, persisted in trying to get away before the appointed time. At last the parish priest knocked him off his horse with a welt of his blackthorn stick and the race started.

We were off like sixteen claps of thunder. We had to circle the field three times, that big field above the beach at Coillnamhan, and before we had circled it the second time, the bay stallion and the mare were in front with the rest nowhere. Neck to neck we ran, and no matter how I urged the mare she would not leave the stallion. Then in the third round of the field I caught a sight of Mary looking at me with a sneer on her face, as if she thought I was afraid to beat the priest's horse. That look drove me mad. I forgot myself. We were stretching towards the winning-post. The stallion was reaching in front of me. Mad with rage I struck the mare a heavy blow between the ears. I had never struck her in my life, and as soon as I had done it I started with

OVERSTEPPING THE LIMIT

fright and shame. I had struck my horse. I spoke to her gently but she just shivered from the tip of her ears to her tail and darted forward with one mighty rush that left the stallion behind.

I heard a shout from the people. I forgot the blow. I forgot the mare. I leaned forward on her mane and yelled myself. We passed the winning-post, with the stallion one hundred yards or more behind us. I tried to draw rein. Her head was like a firm rock. I cursed her and drew rein again. I might have been a flea biting her back. At one bound she leapt the fence and swept down the beach. She was headed straight for the boulders. I saw them in front of me and grew terrified. Between us and the boulders was the sand-bank, fifteen feet high. She snorted, raised her head, and tried to stop when she saw the fall. I heard a shout from the people. Then I became limp. We rose in the air. We fell. The mare struck the rocks and I remembered no more.

They told me afterwards that she was shattered to a pulp when they found us, and sure it's the good God that only gave me a broken leg.

Liam O'Flaherty

OVERSTEPPING THE LIMIT

Suggested activities

1 Did you enjoy the story, or not? Do you think that the story is best listened to, or read silently to yourself? Discuss with a friend how you think that the story should be read; if you think that the story is best read aloud, choose one or two paragraphs and practise reading them to each other, or read them onto a tape recorder and see how they sound.

2 The story is really an account given by one man. Although he tells us what other people said to him, we do not actually hear their voices. All the information comes through Dan of the Fury and we only see what happens from his point of view. We all give clues about ourselves and our opinions in the way we speak and what we speak about. Dan is no exception.

a What clues does Dan give us about himself? For example, you might decide that he likes whisky because of the comments he makes. Find these comments, and find other clues which suggest the sort of person he is, what his opinions are, and how he behaves towards other people. Do this work in pairs if you like, but remember to note down your conclusions clearly.

b When you have decided what Dan might have been like, imagine that you are the stranger to whom he is telling the story; describe Dan carefully as he appears to you. Write this on your own.

3

a Find and write down two sentences, one from lines 41–61 and another from lines 115–28, which suggest that the story will not have a happy ending.

b Write briefly about anything else in lines 1–138 which suggests to you that the ending will not be a happy one.

4 The way in which the last short paragraph is written contrasts with that of the paragraph which precedes it. Try to identify some of the differences and suggest reasons for the different ways in which words are used and the sentences constructed.

5 Imagine that you are *either* Mary *or* Shemus and give your personal account of the day of the races. Try to include some clues as to your own personality and your opinions about Dan and the horse.

6 The background against which a writer sets a story can sometimes affect the story itself. Find the answers to the following questions.

a Where do the events of this story take place?

OVERSTEPPING THE LIMIT

    b What general impressions do you get of the people and the community to which they belong?

    c Do you get any particular impressions of the people from their unusual names?

    d Why do you think that Dan refers to the God Crom?

    e What is Dan's attitude to the priest?

    When you have done this, explain what importance the setting seems to have in the story 'The Black Mare'. Would the story have been any different if it had been set, for example, in another country, or near to a town?

7 Explain what you think is meant or suggested by the following:

    a the flesh on her ribs was as scarce as hospitality in a priest's house (*lines 9–10*)

    b I cared for her as a mother might care for an only child (*line 17*)

    c like a horse from the stable of the God Crom (*lines 37–8*)

    d the craven son of a reptile that he was (*line 72*)

    e She darted forward like a flash of lightning from a darkened sky. (*lines 85–6*)

8 Pick out three similes and three metaphors used in the story and explain why you think that each of them is or is not effective. (Turn to page 132 for help on work with similes and metaphors.)

Suggestions for further creative work

9 'The Black Mare' was told by a man with a distinctive manner of speaking. He used the sayings and rhythms of the everyday speech of his area while he talked. Do you know a dialect or speech style in your area which has special sayings and words? If so, discuss the use of that speech with your friends and see if you can either retell the story of the black mare, or tell a story about another animal, in that style of speech.

10 Discuss what you think was meant by 'But it's an old saying, talk of beauty to-day, talk of death to-morrow.' (*line 40*). Think of other sayings you know which suggest a similar meaning, and make a short collection of them. Choose one and use it as a title for a story of your own; if you do not know of any other sayings, use this one as a title instead.

OVERSTEPPING THE LIMIT

'The Black Mare' is about a man's relationship with a horse, and it ends with his feelings of guilt about striking and destroying the horse. In the following poem, 'First Blood', some people are using a gun for the first time. At first they are very pleased with themselves, but when they kill a squirrel, their mood changes.

First Blood

It was. The breech smelling of oil,
the stock of resin — buried snug
in the shoulder. Not too much recoil
at the firing of the first slug

(jubilantly into the air)   5
nor yet too little. Targets pinned
against a tree: shot down: and there
abandoned to the sniping wind.

My turn first to carry the gun.
Indian file and camouflaged   10
with contours of green shade and sun
we ghosted between larch and larch.

A movement between branches — thump
of a fallen cone. The barrel
jumps, making branches jump   15
higher, dislodging the squirrel

to the next tree. Your turn, my turn.
The silhouette retracts its head.
A hit. 'Let's go back to the lawn.'
'We can't leave it carrying lead   20

for the rest of its life. Reload.
Finish him off. Reload again.'
It was now *him*, and when he showed
the sky cracked like a window pane.

He broke away: traversed a full   25
half dozen trees: vanished. Had found
a hole? We watched that terrible
slow spiral to the clubbing ground.

OVERSTEPPING THE LIMIT

His back was to the tree. His eyes
were gun barrels. He was dumb,   30
and we could not see past the size
of his hands or hear for the drum

in his side. Four shots point-blank
to dull his eyes, a fifth to stop
the shiver in his clotted flank.   35
A fling of earth. As we stood up

the larches closed their ranks. And when
earth would not muffle the drumming blood
we, like dishonoured soldiers, ran
the gauntlet of a darkening wood.   40

Jon Stallworthy

Work with a partner in answering these questions.

11 For each verse of the poem, read the verse separately, then, working together, compose a sentence explaining what is happening.

12 Who are the people in the poem? Their mood changes as the poem develops. In the first verse, they seem to be *curious* about the gun itself; perhaps they have not used a gun before. See if you can think of your own word or phrase which tells us about their mood in the second verse, and then the other verses in turn.

13 Select a phrase from verse 6 which suggests a change in attitude to the squirrel. Why do you think that the poet uses these words? How has their attitude changed?

14 What do you think that the poet suggests by the following? Pay particular attention to the words in italics.

a   and there abandoned to the *sniping* wind. (*lines 7–8*)

b   we *ghosted* between larch and larch, (*line 12*)

c   when he showed the sky *cracked like a window pane*. (*lines 23–4*)
(Does this simile tell us something about the sky, the firing of the gun, the people with the gun, or all three?)

d   We watched that terrible slow spiral to the *clubbing ground*. (*lines 27–8*)

e   The larches *closed their ranks*. (*lines 37*)

f   we, like *dishonoured soldiers*, ran the *gauntlet* of a darkening wood. (*lines 39–40*)

OVERSTEPPING THE LIMIT

15 How does the way in which they see the trees in the last verse differ from the way they responded to them in verse three?

16 What do you think is the significance of the title of this poem?

When you and your partner have completed these questions, compare your answers with those of other members of the class.
The next questions could be attempted working in small groups or on your own.

17 Make up a conversation which they might have had later that evening or the next day. (See page 44 for notes on setting out conversation.)

18 Imagine that you are a close friend of one of the people in the poem. What would you have said and done when you discovered that your friend had killed the squirrel?

19 The killing of the squirrel, and the treatment of the horse in the story, could be described as cruel and thoughtless. There are many examples of good or bad treatment of animals which appear in the newspapers and on television. Cut out examples of such stories and advertisements from any newspapers and magazines available, and arrange them in a folder. Write a short introduction to this folder, describing the contents and giving your views about them. Say whether you think they are exaggerated or sentimental.

20 **either**
Plan and write a letter to a newspaper about the treatment of animals. You may base your letter on one of the newspaper extracts you used in question 19 if you wish.

or
Plan and arrange a series of items and comments which could be put together for a radio or television documentary programme about the treatment of animals. You may want to include imaginary 'guests' to give their views as part of the discussion. Try to achieve some balance of different points of view. If you have done this as a group activity you could actually make the programme and tape-record it.

21 At the end of the poem, 'First Blood', the writer suggests that the people feel guilty about what they have done. Discuss, or write down two or three paragraphs on:

a   The sorts of things which make you feel guilty.

b   The actions of other people which you think *should* make them feel guilty.

EPILOGUE

♦

There is a wide range of poems and stories in this book. Is there any one particular piece which is your favourite? During the course of writing the book, the authors read a great many pieces which obviously could not all be included. Here are two final poems which the authors like. What do you think of them?

Inversnaid

This darksome burn, horseback brown,
His rollrock highroad roaring down,
In coop and in comb the fleece of his foam
Flutes and low to the lake falls home.

A windpuff-bonnet of fawn-froth   5
Turns and twindles over the broth
Of a pool so pitchblack, fell-frowning,
It rounds and rounds Despair to drowning.

Degged with dew, dappled with dew
Are the groins of the braes that the brook treads through,   10
Wiry heathpacks, flitches of fern,
And the beadbonny ash that sits over the burn.

What would the world be, once bereft
Of wet and wildness? Let them be left,
O let them be left, wildness and wet;   15
Long live the weeds and the wilderness yet.

Gerard Manley Hopkins

EPILOGUE

Preludes

I

The winter evening settles down
With smell of steaks in passageways.
Six o'clock.
The burnt-out ends of smoky days.
And now a gusty shower wraps
The grimy scraps
Of withered leaves about your feet
And newspapers from vacant lots;
The showers beat
On broken blinds and chimney-pots,
And at the corner of the street
A lonely cab-horse steams and stamps.
And then the lighting of the lamps.

II

The morning comes to consciousness
Of faint stale smells of beer
From the sawdust-trampled street
With all its muddy feet that press
To early coffee-stands.
With the other masquerades
That time resumes,
One thinks of all the hands
That are raising dingy shades
In a thousand furnished rooms.

III

You tossed a blanket from the bed,
You lay upon your back, and waited;
You dozed, and watched the night revealing
The thousand sordid images
Of which your soul was constituted;
They flickered against the ceiling.
And when all the world came back
And the light crept up between the shutters
And you heard the sparrows in the gutters,
You had such a vision of the street
As the street hardly understands:

EPILOGUE

Sitting along the bed's edge, where 35
You curled the papers from your hair,
Or clasped the yellow soles of feet
In the palms of both soiled hands.

IV

His soul stretched tight across the skies
That fade behind a city block, 40
Or trampled by insistent feet
At four and five and six o'clock;
And short square fingers stuffing pipes,
And even newspapers, and eyes
Assured of certain certainties, 45
The conscience of a blackened street
Impatient to assume the world.

I am moved by fancies that are curled
Around these images, and cling:
The notion of some infinitely gentle 50
Infinitely suffering thing.

Wipe your hand across your mouth, and laugh;
The worlds revolve like ancient women
Gathering fuel in vacant lots.

T.S. Eliot